# Human Resource Management

# Human Resource Management

## The NHS: A Case Study

**Frank Burchill**

*and*

**Alice Casey**

First published 1996 by
MACMILLAN PRESS LTD
Houndmills, Basingstoke, Hampshire RG21 6XS
and London
Companies and representatives
throughout the world

ISBN 0–333–60912–3 hardcover
ISBN 0–333–60913–1 paperback

A catalogue record for this book is available
from the British Library.

10   9   8   7   6   5   4   3   2   1
05   04   03   02   01   00   99   98   97   96

Printed in Hong Kong

# Contents

*To Bernard and Bridie*
*Molly and Peter*

# Abbreviations

| | |
|---|---|
| AAC | Advisory Appointments Committee |
| A&C | administrative and clerical |
| A&E | accident and emergency |
| ACAS | Advisory, Conciliation and Arbitration Service |
| ACB | Association of Clinical Biochemists |
| AEEU | Amalgamated Engineering and Electrical Union |
| AHA | Area Health Authority |
| APEX | Association of Professional, Executive, Clerical and Computer Staff |
| ASC | Ancillary Staff Committee |
| ASTMS | Association of Scientific, Technical and Managerial Staffs |
| AUEW | Amalgamated Union of Engineering Workers |
| BAOT | British Association of Occupational Therapists |
| BDA | British Dental Association |
| BDA | British Dietetic Association |
| BHA | British Hospitals Association |
| BMA | British Medical Association |
| *BMJ* | *British Medical Journal* |
| BOS | British Orthoptic Society |
| BQA | British Quality Association |
| CATS | credit accumulated transfer schemes |
| CBI | Confederation of British Industry |
| CDNA | Community and District Nursing Association |
| CENTEC | Central England Enterprise Council |
| CEO | chief executive officer |
| COHSE | Confederation of Health Service Employees |
| COSHH | Control of Substances Hazardous to Health Regulations 1988 |
| CPSM | Council for the Professions Supplementary to Medicine |
| CRE | Commission for Racial Equality |
| CSP | Chartered Society of Physiotherapists |
| DDRB | Doctors' and Dentists' Review Body |

| | |
|---|---|
| DGH | district general hospital |
| DGM | district general manager |
| DHA | District Health Authority |
| DHSS | Department of Health and Social Security |
| DMT | district management team |
| DMU | directly managed unit |
| DNA | District Nursing Association |
| DOCAS | deduction of contributions at source |
| DOH | Department of Health |
| DPO | district personnel officer |
| EC | European Community |
| EETPU | Electrical, Electronic, Telecommunications and Plumbing Union |
| EL | executive letter |
| EOC | Equal Opportunities Commission |
| EOP | equal opportunities policy |
| EPA | Equal Pay Act 1970 |
| EP(C)A | Employment Protection (Consolidation) Act 1978 |
| EU | European Union |
| EVA | Equal Value Amendment 1983 |
| FCE | finished consultant episode |
| FTE | full time equivalent |
| GDC | General Dental Council |
| GMB | GMB Union |
| GMBATU | General Municipal, Boilermakers and Allied Trades Union |
| GMC | General Medical Council |
| GNP | gross national product |
| GP | general practitioner |
| GPF | general practitioner fundholder |
| GWC | General Whitley Council |
| HCA | health care assistant |
| HCHS | hospital and community health services |
| HCSA | Hospital Consultants' and Specialists' Association |
| HPA | Hospital Physicists Association |
| HR | human resource |
| HRM | human resource management |
| HSC | Health and Safety Commission |
| HSCC | hospital staff consultative committee |
| HSE | Health and Safety Executive |

| | |
|---|---|
| HSWA | Health and Safety etc at Work Act 1974 |
| HVA | Health Visitors' Association |
| IHSM | Institute of Health Service Management |
| ILO | International Labour Organisation |
| IPD | Institute of Personnel and Development |
| IR | industrial relations |
| JCC | joint consultative committee |
| JIT | just-in-time |
| JNC | joint negotiating committee |
| JSC | joint staff committee |
| JSCC | joint staff consultative committee |
| JSSC | joint shop stewards committee |
| LEU | local employment unit |
| MHSWR | Management of Health and Safety at Work Regulations 1992 |
| MLSO | medical laboratory scientific officer |
| MSF | Manufacturing, Science and Finance |
| NAHAT | National Association of Health Authorities and Trusts |
| NAHA | National Association of Health Authorities |
| NALGO | National and Local Government Officers Association |
| NHS | National Health Service |
| NHSE | National Health Service Executive |
| NHSTD | National Health Service Training Directorate/Division |
| NUPE | National Union of Public Employees |
| NVQ | National Vocational Qualification |
| OME | Office of Manpower Economics |
| PAM | professions allied to medicine |
| PBR | payment-by-results |
| PCR | professional contribution rating |
| PES | public expenditure survey |
| PI | performance indicator |
| PM | personnel management |
| POWAR | place of work accredited representatives |
| PRB | pay review body |
| PRP | performance-related pay |
| PT'A' | Professional and Technical Council 'A' |
| PT'B' | Professional and Technical Council 'B' |
| QAT | quality action team |

| | |
|---|---|
| RAWP | resource allocation working party |
| RCM | Royal College of Midwives |
| RCN | Royal College of Nursing |
| RHA | Regional Health Authority |
| RIDDOR | Reporting of Injuries, Diseases and Dangerous Occurrences Regulations 1985 |
| RM | registered midwife |
| RN | registered nurse |
| RO | regional office |
| SEA | Single European Act |
| SEN | state enrolled nurse |
| SGT | self-governing trust |
| SHO | senior house officer |
| SoC | Society of Chiropodists |
| SoR | Society of Radiographers |
| SRN | state registered nurse |
| TGWU | Transport and General Workers Union |
| TQC | total quality control |
| TQI | total quality improvement |
| TQM | total quality management |
| TUC | Trade Union Congress |
| TULR(C)A | Trade Union and Labour Relations (Consolidation) Act 1992 |
| TURERA | Trade Union Reform and Employment Rights Act 1993 |
| UCATT | Union of Construction, Allied Trades and Technicians |
| UGM | unit general manager |
| UKCC | United Kingdom Central Council |
| ULC | unit labour cost |
| UNISON | public sector trade union formed by a merger of COHSE, NALGO and NUPE |
| USDAW | Union of Shop, Distributive and Allied Workers |
| VDU | visual display unit |
| WHO | World Health Organisation |
| WTE | whole time equivalent |

# Introduction

The objective of this book is to provide an introduction to those topics generally associated with the term 'human resource management' (HRM). It is intended that this will be a broad introduction, but linked together by reference to a coherent set of examples of practice applied within the National Health Service. These examples reflect practice at the time of writing. They are not presented in any prescriptive sense, but simply to help illustrate the topics considered and, perhaps, to generate a better understanding of the issues raised.

As a term, HRM is not treated as problematic. It is simply treated as one which is generally replacing 'personnel management' as a title for the area of study under consideration. Current texts with HRM in the title usually end up discussing practice in the three major areas traditionally associated with personnel management texts: resourcing; development; employee relations. Torrington and Hall (1995), which keeps personnel management as its main title, clearly follows this pattern. Storey and Sisson (1993), which has the title 'Managing Human Resources and Industrial Relations', focuses exactly on the same three areas.

This is not to say that all such texts have identical concerns or analyses. The separating out of HRM and industrial relations in the text referred to above is of some significance. According to Storey and Sisson (1993:2), 'personnel management could be traditionally understood as concerned with policies and practices directed towards the *individual* employee, whereas, industrial relations could be suitably regarded as concerned with *collective* labour issues' (italics in original). Torrington and Hall (1991: especially 501–35) have not been inhibited by such a distinction – they include a consideration of collective labour issues. The above comment is also at odds with Clegg (1979:1).

What is industrial relations? The answer which is assumed in this book is that it is the study of the rules governing employment, together with the ways in which rules are made and changed, interpreted and administered. Implicit in this definition is the notion that industrial relations is as concerned with those policies which are directed at the individual as it is with those directed at the collective. It could, however, be argued that the section on collective issues in Torrington and Hall derives from the subject matter of industrial relations and that the distinctive feature of personnel management is its concern with resourcing and development.

There is another distinction. Texts on personnel management are generally prescriptive. They usually attempt to describe 'good' or 'effective' practice. Texts on industrial relations tend to be analytical, have a historical perspective and place emphasis on the importance of power and shifts in its balance. There is no reason why such an analysis should not be applied to the whole field of personnel management. This would lead us to examine what is going on within the three areas of activity and perhaps explore why.

Attempts to identify the substance of HRM usually consist of producing a list of characteristics supposedly describing personnel management/industrial relations (PM/IR) and a contrasting list for HRM (see Storey, 1992:35). In such models we find, for example, that PM/IR tends to be pluralist, HRM, unitarist; the business plan is marginal to PM/IR but central to HRM; 'facilitation' is prized by HRM as a managerial skill rather than 'negotiation', which is favoured by PM/IR, and so on. Similarly, there are 'hard' and 'soft' versions of HRM.

It is possible to argue that in the traditional areas of concern for students of personnel management there have been widespread changes of practice, with common elements, but unevenly distributed. These changes can be primarily located in the 1980s and the 1990s. The interesting questions are: What are these changes? Why have they taken place? Why are there variations? Why do they occur unevenly? Whether a particular combination of changes or practices constitutes HRM as opposed to PM/IR is singularly uninteresting. Hence the lack of concern relating to the title used in this text.

Storey and Sisson (1993:50) say: 'Superficially, given the reduction in overt industrial conflict and the apparent increase in attention to human resource matters by general and line managers as well as personnel specialists, the industrial relations and HR problem might seem to be close to a solution.' As far as the authors of this text are concerned there is no 'problem' and therefore no 'solution'. There are areas of activity and change which are worthy of study. These areas of activity for the purpose of this text are the human resourcing of organisations in industry, the development of staff in these organisations, and what is variously called 'employee', 'labour' or 'industrial' relations. Participants in these activities will perceive both problems and solutions. The origins of such perceptions will need to be examined and placed in the context of wider economic and political considerations.

The NHS has been variously reorganised since its creation in 1948. In 1990, the NHS and Community Care Act was a major step in the radical reforms of the NHS which had progressed throughout the 1980s. This introduced the internal market and brought into full play a whole range of commercial practices generally associated with the private sector. The rhetoric of financial accountability was used to put pressure on NHS costs and in particular labour costs. Compulsory competitive tendering had already preceded this development. These changes put tremendous pressure on the general employment and HRM practices of employing units, such as hospitals and community units, as they became trusts and are judged by financial criteria.

Paralleling these developments were general pressures from the National Health Service Executive (NHSE) to mimic the HRM practices of the private sector. NHS trusts, to varying degrees, have absorbed the practice of issuing mission statements, talking about total quality and world excellence, introducing performance-related pay and attempting the range of flexibilities in terms of employment practices. The dismantling of Whitley and the pay review bodies have drawn trusts into local pay determination. So far, trusts have generally held back from derecognition of unions. Whether this is to facilitate the shorter-run changes remains to be seen.

This book has been written in the midst of wholesale change in the NHS. It examines the range of HRM policies of a trust. The objective is to provide a case study which allows background and theoretical analysis of such policies to be given practical content. As such, the text should be of use to general students of the subject. It also chronicles the experiences of a trust in this important period of NHS development.

The text is structured in such a way that it allows for the statement of basic HRM principles which are then related to practice in a trust. This is therefore a general text on HRM with practical examples which follow in an integrated fashion. It begins with human resource planning, a topic which allows for an overview of the subject of HRM and the organisation under consideration. This is followed by some examination of the debate relating to the meaning of HRM which is used to provide a device for introducing a discussion of current management practices and their origins. Most of what follows the Chapter 2 section on current management practices is relatively straightforward. For teaching purposes, a chapter has been included which contains case studies. This is very much rooted in changes taking place at the time of writing and in particular the development of bargaining. It is the authors' view that the issues arising, and the effects on practice, will continue for a long time to be of importance, not only in the NHS, but in other industries also.

FRANK BURCHILL
ALICE CASEY

## Acknowledgements

The authors and publishers are grateful to the following for permission to reproduce copyright material: OPCS for Tables 1.1 and A.1 and Figures 1.1, A.3 and A.4; KPMG Management Consulting and Central Manchester Healthcare Trust for Table 11.1; and NAHAT for Figures A.1, A.2 and A.5.

# 1

# Human Resource Planning

This chapter is concerned with the way in which managers in an organisation decide the numbers and types, in terms of skills and abilities, of people it needs to employ directly or indirectly in order to secure business objectives, and how they set about achieving this. The NHS uses a particularly complex labour force and this is a consequence of the nature of its activities. Table 1.1 breaks down the directly employed staff of the NHS into its main groups. Figure 1.1 shows trends in these groups.

At the point of production staffing is intimately bound up with costs and revenues. Anticipated revenues can be turned into a budget which sets cost limits to staffing. The revenues will be linked to an anticipated range of activities designed to secure them. This range of activities will incur investment costs, depreciation charges and land costs on top of the human resource costs. Investment in new technology will have implications for the mix of skills required of the human resources. It is estimated that staffing costs account for just over two-thirds of total NHS expenditure (OPCS, 1995).

**The Business Plan**

A human resource strategy must be linked to a business plan for the unit of production. A business plan costs in detail a business strategy. This is the logic of human resource planning. Storey and Sisson (1993:ch. 3) provide an excellent critique of this kind of analysis, and a review of the associated literature. Nothing is ever so simple is their effective conclusion. Part of the difficulty is that the term 'strategy' itself is so problematic. Where does such a thing begin and end? People and organisations certainly have

TABLE 1.1  NHS staff in post, by main group[1]

| Whole time equivalents staff group | 1983 | 1986 | 1987 | 1988 | 1989 | 1990 | 1991 | 1992 | 1993 | Percentage change 1983–93 |
|---|---|---|---|---|---|---|---|---|---|---|
| Nursing midwifery (including agency) | 397 100 | 402 700 | 404 000 | 403 900 | 405 300 | 402 100 | 396 100 | 382 000 | 366 200 | −7.8 |
| % of all staff | 47.8 | 50.2 | 50.5 | 50.9 | 50.9 | 50.5 | 49.5 | 48.0 | 47.3 | |
| Medical and dental[2] (including locum) | 42 300 | 43 300 | 43 500 | 44 800 | 46 300 | 47 400 | 48 600 | 49 600 | 51 100 | 20.9 |
| % of all staff | 5.1 | 5.4 | 5.4 | 5.6 | 5.8 | 5.9 | 6.1 | 6.2 | 6.6 | |
| All professional and technical[3,4] (excluding works) | 68 700 | 76 100 | 79 300 | 79 800 | 81 200 | 84 000 | 86 900 | 89 800 | 91 100 | 32.7 |
| % of all staff | 8.3 | 9.5 | 9.9 | 10.1 | 10.2 | 10.5 | 10.9 | 11.3 | 11.8 | |
| Ancillary | 166 200 | 124 300 | 115 100 | 107 600 | 102 400 | 95 700 | 85 500 | 79 000 | 77 800 | −53.2 |
| % of all staff | 20.0 | 15.5 | 14.4 | 13.6 | 12.9 | 12.0 | 10.7 | 9.9 | 10.0 | |
| Administration and clerical | 110 000 | 110 800 | 113 900 | 114 700 | 116 800 | 120 000 | 127 400 | 135 000 | 132 600 | 20.6 |
| % of all staff | 13.3 | 13.8 | 14.2 | 14.5 | 14.7 | 15.1 | 15.9 | 17.0 | 17.1 | |
| Maintenance and works | 26 800 | 25 000 | 24 200 | 22 700 | 21 200 | 19 900 | 18 300 | 17 900 | 16 700 | −37.8 |
| % of all staff | 3.2 | 3.1 | 3.0 | 2.9 | 2.7 | 2.5 | 2.3 | 2.3 | 2.2 | |
| General/senior management[5] | n/a | 500 | 700 | 1 200 | 4 600 | 9 700 | 14 500 | 17 700 | 20 000 | |
| % of all staff | | 0.1 | 0.1 | 0.2 | 0.6 | 1.2 | 1.8 | 2.2 | 2.6 | |

| | | | | | | | | | | % change |
|---|---|---|---|---|---|---|---|---|---|---|
| Ambulance (including officers)[4] | 18 400 | 19 000 | 19 000 | 18 800 | 18 900 | 18 100 | 17 600 | 17 700 | 17 500 | −4.9 |
| % of all staff | 2.2 | 2.4 | 2.4 | 2.4 | 2.4 | 2.3 | 2.2 | 2.2 | 2.3 | |
| Others[5] | — | — | — | — | — | — | 4 900 | 6 300 | 800 | |
| % of all staff | — | — | — | — | — | — | 0.6 | 0.8 | 0.1 | |
| Total employed staff | 829 500 | 801 600 | 799 300 | 796 600 | 796 900 | 800 200 | 795 100 | 773 900 | 17 500 | −6.7 |

*Notes*

1. At 30 September, includes staff at the Dental Practice Board, Prescriptions Pricing Authority, Special Health Authorities and Family Health Service Authorities. From 1987 onwards, figures also include the Other Statutory Authorities (e.g. PILS and HEA) not previously collected in the annual workforce consensus. Figures are therefore not comparable with those from earlier years. All figures are also subsequently rounded to the nearest. Whole-time equivalents. Percentages are calculated on unrounded figures. Figures exclude independent family health service contractors and practice staff directly employed by them.

2. Includes all permanent paid and honorary staff in hospitals and community health services, hospital practitioners and part-time medical/dental officers.

3. Not adjusted for transfer of operating department assistants from Ancillary to Professional & Technical staff groups on 1 April 1984.

4. Validation of the 1993 data for Scientific & Professional and Ambulance staff uncovered errors in the 1992 data. These errors have been corrected in the above table.

5. A change in data collection procedures in September 1993 resulted in their categorisation of many staff who would have been classed as 'others' in the 1991 and 1992 consensus. To put the 1993 figures in their correct context, amended figures have been estimated for 1991 and 1992. These differ from figures published as previous departmental reports. The trend in management numbers between 1990 and 1993 is unaffected by these adjustments.

*Source* OPCS (1995).

FIGURE 1.1   *Indices of staff in post, by main staff group*

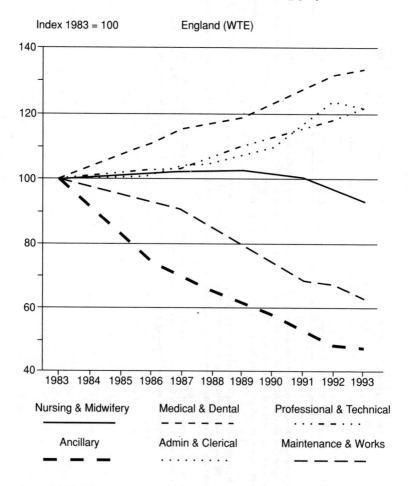

Source: OPCS (1995).

time perspectives in respect of particular activities. Annual budgets are a common phenomenon and these cannot exist in a vacuum. As far as the NHS is concerned, widespread integrated changes have taken place, ranging from the introduction of general management to the introduction of the so-called 'internal market'.

All units of production face markets in the sense that the forces of supply and demand affect their activities. The recession of the last 20 years has generally led to the view that expansion is a zero sum game – market gains are competitors' losses. Strategic planning usually revolves around identifying the general political, economic, social and technological forces at play (PEST analysis) and then linking these to the specific strengths, weaknesses, opportunities and threats (SWOT analysis) possessed and faced by the organisation. The search is for strategic advantage over competitors.

Whatever the process used, each unit of production will operate within a *plan*, or, if autonomous, develop its own. In other words, there will be what is generally referred to as a *corporate strategy*. Each unit will need to link its strategy to this. What it does and plans to do will be constrained by the corporate plan or strategy. It follows that component parts of units – the finance department, estates department and HRM department, for example – will equally need to fit their strategies to that of the unit. All of these plans and strategies will be buffeted by circumstances and events often outside the control of the organisation or sections within it.

This chapter is concerned with human resource planning. Other chapters will deal with development and employee relations. A human resource strategy will link all three to the corporate plan. What follows is a case study which examines human resource planning at the level of a NHS hospital trust.

## Human Resource Planning in a NHS Hospital Trust

*The General Context*

What are called NHS trusts were established in the UK in 1991. The day-to-day operations of the NHS are managed by the National Health Service Executive (NHSE). The NHSE operates within strategy determined by the Department of Health Policy Board which is chaired by the Secretary of State. Trusts are expected to provide both hospital and community health services. They govern themselves, but are directly responsible to the NHSE. (See Figure A.4 in the appendix.)

The hospital trust in question (our trust) is governed by a Trust Board which consists of a chairman, five non-executive directors and seven executive directors. Statute requires that there be no more than five voting executive directors. These five must include the Chief Executive, medical director, finance director and nurse director. The chairman and three of the non-executive directors are appointed by the Secretary of State for Health, with the two other non-executive directors appointed by the regional office. At least two of the non-executive directors must be female. In our trust, the three additional directors come from personnel, facilities and business development. It is important to note that personnel is not seen to have an automatic role at board level.

The key responsibilities of the board are described as:

1. determining the strategy and policies of the trust,
2. developing the trust business plan,
3. monitoring the implementation of trust strategies, policies and business plans,
4. maintaining the financial viability of the trust.

Provision of health care services takes place within a clinical directorate structure. There are seven clinical directorates which cover general medicine and care of the elderly, obstetrics, gynaecology and paediatrics; theatres and anaesthetics; trauma, orthopaedics and accident and emergency; general surgery, urology and ear nose and throat; pathology; radiology. Each of these areas is led by a clinical director (see Figure 1.2).

In HRM terms the notion of a clinical directorate is important. It reflects a central NHS strategic objective of involving clinicians in management. This is based on a concern that clinical judgements should also be informed by financial considerations. Incorporating clinicians into management decision making was seen as one way of doing this. Clinical directors, with the support of a business manager and a directorate nurse/midwife manager, are responsible for business planning, within allocated budgets, staff and budget management, operational management, agreeing and monitoring quality standards and internal and external service agreements.

FIGURE 1.2 *Trusts*

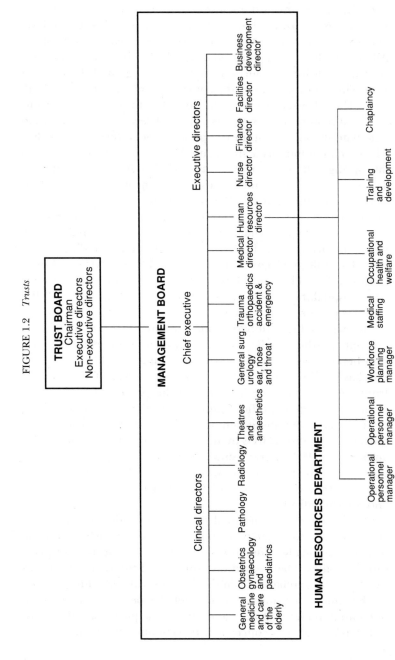

It can be seen from the above that there is an overall business plan at trust board level, seven business plans at directorate level and six executive directors, each with their own business plans. All of these have to be integrated. The key plan is that of the trust board, which for our purposes could be designated the *corporate plan*. This is devised within the context of the overall central NHS plan. The NHS sets itself health care objectives and estimates its financial requirements over a period of three years. It then has to negotiate its budget within the public expenditure survey (PES) which is a continuous activity, running on an annual basis from late spring. These negotiations involve dealing directly with the Treasury. Other departments of state are engaged in making bids at the same time, and the Treasury will be trying to ensure that departmental spending allocations match overall government economic strategies. Whatever the general impact of the balance of arguments used is, the NHS will be granted a funding allocation. This will then have to be distributed by the NHS and decisions taken at this level will ultimately cascade downwards to our trust hospital, becoming the major determining factor in all the business plans referred to above.

The National Health Service and Community Care Act of 1990 not only produced self-governing trusts, it also created the division between *purchasers* and *providers*. Funds are allocated to the purchasers who then buy health care on behalf of the patients from the providers. The first stage of this process of allocation is to the eight regional offices (ROs). Allocations to ROs are based on a formula combining demographic, morbidity and social factors in the weighting. ROs then make allocations to district health authorities (DHAs), also using a formula system. The DHAs are the major purchasers of the sevices available from the providers. Other purchasers include GP fundholders, private companies and private individuals.

In this context our hospital trust is a provider of services in competition with other trusts both in the district and, for some services, nationally. Human resource planning has to take place within business plans based on estimates of the value of services which will be purchased from the Trust over the planning period. At the time of writing, approximately 94 per cent of potential purchasing power is in the hands of a single purchaser, the DHA, as far as our trust is concerned. In economic terms this is what would be called a highly monopsonistic market. (In economics the term 'monopsony' is used to describe a situation where there is only a single purchaser of a product.) This purchaser is also acting as a proxy for the patient, or consumer. DHAs are encouraged to merge or collaborate to rationalise purchases across boundaries.

Although the trust is directly responsible to the Secretary of State, its performance is monitored by the RO. Through the RO, the trust is expected to submit to the NHSE an annual business plan. This plan must detail the services it expects to provide, its capital investment programme and any new developments. Obviously the content of this plan must indicate the contracts the trust expects to secure from the purchasers. Notionally the trust will be in competition with other providers in trying to secure contracts. NHS trusts are subjected to nationally determined financial objectives. They must (1) achieve a break-even position on an income and expenditure basis, (2) meet a 6 per cent rate of return on capital employed, and (3) keep within a required external financial limit – basically a limit on borrowing.

It has to be acknowledged that competition in the NHS is not free competition – it is managed competition. Central NHS objectives are never totally explicit in detail. New technology is creating a need for more day case interventions and therefore fewer hospital beds (other things being equal). The NHSE is aiming at 60 per cent of all elective surgery being performed as day cases by 1997/8. Following from this would be a fall in the demand for hospital beds and perhaps a need for fewer hospitals. Purchasers will be expected to force through a strategy aimed at altering the distribution of hospitals, their size and location. Providers who are currently seen to be relatively efficient will become less efficient in the context of a small number of large hospitals and a large number of community practices. Competition creates uncertainties; managed competition introduces 'wild cards'. Business plans can never adequately cater for the impact of both.

In the short run, change, generally, but not always, for both purchasers and providers will be incremental. Purchasers need to arrange their contracts in such a way that the communities they serve receive adequate health care provision. This will mean that

providers will be bidding for contracts on the basis of their previous provision of services, with some developments. Human
resource planning will take place within this context. It will rarely
take place in an environment which allows a completely fresh
start.

### The HRM Context

The NHSE contains seven directorates, one of which is personnel. Human resource planning at the level of the trust has to take
account of HRM policy determined at NHSE level. The NHS is a
signatory to Opportunity 2000 and the NHSE has set targets for
female employment (NHSE, 1992). For example, its first goal is
stated as: 'Increase the number of women in general management posts from 18 per cent in 1991 to 30 per cent in 1994.' (See
Chapter 6 for a discussion of legislation.) It lays down similar
objectives for the employment of women accountants, of women
consultants, women members of authorities and trusts, and retention strategies following career breaks.

Other national personnel objectives also have to be taken
account of in the process of human resource planning at the
level of our trust. The NHSE has referred to all the following in
EL(94)55, *Priorities and planning guidance for the NHS: 1995/96.*

* reduction in junior doctors' hours,
* skill mix,
* use of subcontracted labour,
* nurse prescribing,
* paying for performance,
* flexibility in hours and pay,
* flexibility of function.

Other items in the list of priorities clearly impinge on HRM planning.

Many of these issues are discussed in future chapters. Overall,
human resource managers are expected to demonstrate a concern for improving productivity by the use of the whole range of
current management practices. The purchasers will examine the
employment practices of the providers to ensure that they are

attempting to be as efficient as possible. Business plans will be expected to predict efficiency savings and sources of income generation, all of which have human resourcing implications.

*A Trust Human Resource Plan*

Texts on human resource planning tend to work within a basic demand and supply model. In the case of our trust, it will have a demand for human resources which is derived from its level of activity. At a very crude level, if the level of activity were predicted to increase by 10 per cent all round, 10 per cent more staff might be required. Economies of scale or changes in technology obviously undermine such a crude approach. According to Armstrong (1990:126), managerial judgement is the typical method used:

> It simply means that you sit down, think about future developments and workloads and then decide how many and what sort of people you need. The judgement may be based on rules of thumb about the relationship between activity levels and the requirement for people, plus a broad assessment of the impact of technological and other developments on human resource requirements. Essentially, however, it is guesswork.

An implication of the above is that all employers will have a forecast of the future demand for human resources, but some will be more carefully thought through than others. Using various statistical techniques to extrapolate from past experience will inevitably contain judgements: the future is never going to be perfectly predictable, even in this limited area of activity. Even if a predicted level of activity does not materialise, it should be possible to link different levels of activity to specific combinations of human resource inputs, while recognising that technology and other factors might change these ratios.

In a text such as this it is only worth stating the fact that there are refined forecasting techniques used in this field – see Armstrong (1990:ch. 8), Storey and Sisson (1993:ch. 5), IMS (1993). Here we are concerned with a case study. The human resource plan of our trust was complicated by the fact that the provision of services was being moved into a newly built hospital. On the basis of the services plan it was predicted that the new district general hospital (DGH) would employ 1339 full-time equivalents. These would be distributed within the following staff categories:

| | |
|---|---|
| Nursing and midwives, including students | 49 per cent |
| Medical staff | 9 per cent |
| Administrative and clerical | 14 per cent |
| Ancillary | 11 per cent |
| Estates | 3 per cent |
| Professional and technical | 14 per cent |

The key indicators of the trust hospital's performance were established as:

1. monthly indicators of finished consultant episodes (FCEs) and attendances of consultants against contracts;
2. theatre utilisation;
3. average length of stay;
4. available and occupied bed days;
5. percentage day cases.

Targets set within these indicators have implications for human resource planning. Achievements elsewhere against such indicators are available nationally, and the NHSE has targets. A responsibility of the personnel department was to establish a manpower (HR) plan and a recruitment process to match the corporate plan. It also had to ensure that all consultants had job plans in line with FCE targets.

A consequence of the opening of the new DGH was that allowance had been made for increased activities. A 24-hour accident and emergency service was to be provided, and other additional acute services, including a paediatric ward and an intensive care unit. Again the human resource plan had to take account of these. The financial plan contained the following total revenue budget:

| | Current Year £m | Year 1 £m | Year 2 £m |
|---|---|---|---|
| Pay costs | 17.5 | 20.3 | 20.7 |
| Non-pay | 6.4 | 7.8 | 9.5 |
| Capital charges | 2.1 | 3.6 | 5.3 |

Before considering recruitment to meet additional services an effective HR plan required a thorough examination of the current utilisation of existing human resources, along with possible alternatives to direct employment. The personnel department had to analyse its own activities to be tested against the market: could all or any of its services be bought in at a more economic cost?

The largest human resource cost was incurred by nursing and midwifery activities. The efficiency of these activities, as currently performed in the hospital, was examined using classic Taylorite techniques (see Chapter 2 ). In the NHS the terms used for such techniques tend to be *work profiling* and *skill mix analysis*. These terms are used interchangeably, and could be replaced by the more traditional term, *work study*. According to the British Standards Institution (1969):

> Work study is a generic term for these techniques, particularly *method study* and *work measurement*, which are used in the examination of human work in all its contexts, and which lead systematically to the investigation of all the factors which affect the efficiency and economy of the situation being reviewed, in order to effect improvement.

At a very basic level what was required was knowledge of the precise tasks that nursing and midwifery staff performed; how frequently these tasks were performed, along with daily and other periodic fluctuations; the time spent on performing tasks, and so on. Caseloads could be identified and related to measures of patient dependency – some patients require more care than others. It was recognised that there were variations in what could be described as the relationship between workloads and staff ratios. These often varied between shifts. Part of the study involved examining the mix of skills of staff in relation to equivalent workloads. Here it was found that with identical workloads there were different mixes of higher and lower graded staff along with mixes of clinical and non-clinical staff. Often clinical staff were undertaking non-clinical tasks – bed making, for example.

The above kind of analysis is systematic rather than scientific. It could provide arguments for more flexible shift patterns and less costly mixes of staff. However it does raise questions. Quality of care, or outcomes, is difficult to measure. Taking non-clinical work away from clinicians increases the intensity of their work.

Shortening shift overlaps does the same. There is no obvious method of identifying ideal staff/workload relationships.

A variety of methods tends to be brought to bear to supplement work study in order to try to identify apropriate levels and mixes of staff in relation to the the workload. *Professional judgement* relies on a professional at the point of production offering an estimate of the staff input required. *Norms* can emanate from the professional bodies themselves who may, for example, lay down the number of midwife WTEs required for size of unit, or in relation to number of births. *Inequality regressions* is an elaborate term to describe staffing levels required based on projections of comparisons of averages for a comparable group of hospitals. The IMS (1993:27) identify ratios as the most frequently used method in the NHS for establishing staffing levels. These are established at regional or district level on the basis of advice, negotiations and historical relationships, and enforced at unit level. This is known as a *top-down* method. Purchasers may use their power to enforce such ratios on trusts.

A more detailed account of these methods as used in the NHS is given in IMS (1993:s. 1.5). The principles applied are obvious, but the complexity of work and the difficulties involved in measuring quality in the NHS raise a lot of questions about the ultimate validity of any or all of the processes used separately or combined. Local demographic factors and morbidity rates affect comparisons, as do internal factors: the quality of management, technology and so on. Although there will be a 'regression to norms', the use of the above techniques provides arguments to be used in negotiations with those affected in order to try to generate increased productivity and force down costs. The power of management will vary in relation to the power of those supplying the services and thus the outcomes of negotiations will vary from place to place and over time. Research has indicated that the quality of care is better, the higher the grade of nurses who provide it, and the higher the grade mix, the better the care provided by lower grades (Carr-Hill *et al.*, 1992).

The above has been concerned with the demand for labour – estimating the volume of labour required on the basis of predicted output levels, previous relationships and the perceived efficiency of the labour force and what is coming to be called the 're-engineering' of that labour force. Once an establishment has been planned, the supply of labour to match that establishment has to be secured. There is no doubt that the basic methodology used above is of wider application. Its main ingredients are extensively used for establishing HR plans. Where we are dealing with physical units of output and widely available technologies, variations in productivity can be directly compared. Womack *et al.* (1990), can examine the number of labour hours used to assemble a car, the number of defects per 100 cars and the average number of square feet of factory space per car, and make performance comparisons between plants that allow for obvious conclusions. The same can be done in other areas of manufacturing. The NHS is more complex, and the reasons for this are obvious. Nevertheless some basis has to be found for justifying expenditures on human resources in the NHS, even if it were to provide treatment free at the point of delivery on a completely open basis.

Other aspects of manipulating the demand for labour are dealt with in Chapter 11, particularly in respect of flexibility. Absenteeism control can also be used in attempts to reduce the demand for labour, along with other factors relating to lateness, holiday entitlements and so on.

### The Supply of Labour

Securing a supply of labour for a greenfield site is clearly different from planning the future of a brownfield site or, as in the case of our trust, an element of both. It is also going to be different with a complex labour force. Establishing the demand side is more difficult to achieve than dealing with the supply side. In fact, the business plan will have incorporated costings which already acknowledge supply-side problems. The estimated cost of providing a specialism will have taken account of the scarcities or otherwise of the required specialists, and their pay. A careful analysis and manipulation of the supply side will help to minimise costs.

Work study, as described above, could be seen as reducing the demand for additional labour by making more effective use of the existing labour force. On the other hand, it could be seen as increasing the available supply of labour by releasing underemployed labour to take on new tasks. Both of these processes, other things being equal, work to reduce the cost of labour – the cost of human resources. This suggests that there are internal sources of supply as well as external sources.

*Internal Labour Market.* Work study and skill mix analysis could lead to redeployment of labour. The introduction of health care assistants (HCAs) into the NHS provided a generic category of labour which could be employed and trained within the National Vocational Qualification (NVQ) structure within all categories of employment in the NHS. At the lowest level they could be used to take on non-clinical tasks from nursing staff, or lower grade clerical tasks.

Other internal sources would include promotions, introduction of skill flexibilities and working on labour turnover to improve retention of existing qualified or unqualified staff. People may leave to work for other employers or they may leave for career breaks. The NHS is a significant employer of part-time labour. This can introduce an attractive form of flexibility, but needs to be used in a cost-effective way. Child care provision can help retain labour and so also could proper provision for return to work after career breaks.

Providing such benefits incurs costs. Annual budgeting might result in short-term decisions being made in these areas. The recession has forced down labour turnover rates and recently reduced vacancy rates for qualified staff (Nursing and Midwifery Staffside, 1993). Absenteeism might be reduced by control systems or 'healthy employee' strategies (see Chapter 5). These will be less costly in terms of annual budgets, but could create longer term problems by simply suppressing discontent behind low morale. The same could be true if increased productivity of the existing labour force were secured by increased work intensity, with its corollary of increased stress.

Chapter 2 discusses relevant aspects of current management practices. The NHS approach to management is being influenced by that of other industries. Oliver and Wilkinson (1992) point to K-Electric often requiring its employees to work between two and four hours' overtime a day. There is evidence that other companies do this (Toyota:Wales; Rover – see Casey, 1993). Recruiting to below known staffing requirements and using overtime is a way of improving security of employment at the expense of more intensive work arrangements.

*External Labour Market.* The external labour market might be used to recruit both core and peripheral labour. Again, a peripheral labour force might be used to deal with work fluctuations. This relates to numerical flexibility. See Chapter 11 for definitions of these terms. The scale of the external labour market is linked to the type of staff required. For our trust, the search for a paediatrics consultant was virtually worldwide. Obviously there is a local, national and international market, and potential sources of supply need to be identified.

A large proportion of the labour force in the NHS is highly trained in highly specialised, industry-specific skills. For these staff the potential supply is well defined. Training costs are high and the sources of new entrants into the national market have been relatively limited. Nursing and medical schools are the major providers. Traditionally these have been hospital and university-based. Hospital training is being transferred to universities through Project 2000. HCAs are seen as partial replacements for student nursing and midwifery staff at the unit level.

Currently purchasers are arranging contracts with the universities to buy the training of nursing staff. It is easy to imagine the contract funding diminishing and the cost of training, as with other university students, being passed on to individuals through student and career development loans. This will privatise a large part of the cost of training, with perhaps the providers of health care – the trusts – offering bursaries when they meet shortages. HCAs will be offered NVQ, Credit Accumulated Transfer Schemes (CATS) based training, with a growth in distance learning packages. This will allow for study in their own time. With the rapid growth of new surgical technology the medical profession will come under pressure to examine boundaries between specialisms. There is already a proposal drastically to reduce the training period for consultants, and access to training is likely to widen.

What the latter comments indicate is that as far as training is concerned there is a national strategy, not explicitly declared but implicit in the range of NHSE initiatives.

**Summary**

It is not possible to attempt a full scale analysis of HR planning in a text such as this. The reader is referred to Waite (1991). It has been suggested in this chapter that HR planning consists of examining the need, as clearly as possible, for the type of labour required – the demand for labour. This involved looking at the activities from which the demand for labour is derived, investigating existing utilisation of labour and possible adjustments to this, and predicting the future as indicated by the corporate plan. Having done this, relevant markets have to be examined to ascertain effective sources of supply, and these markets are both external and internal. References to training, flexibility, work study and so on show that the HR plan will overlap into development and employee relations. This chapter will provide a continuing reference point throughout our study of HRM.

In our trust, the personnel department was responsible for putting together the HR plan based on the corporate plan. Work profiling and skill mix analyses were carried out. Future staffing requirements were identified, and staff were secured from within and without to ensure an establishment for the new hospital. Details and adjustments had to be negotiated with clinical and nursing directors, along with the trust directors. At the time of writing, a 'wild card' came into play. The regional office began by changing from supporting paediatrics provision in the new hospital to opposing such provision. This would have had effects on obstetrics, and the corporate plan, along with all other plans, including the HR plan, would have had to be rewritten. All of these plans had been based on the RO's original intentions. Chapter 9 illustrates the ultimate outcome of RO decisions.

From the very beginning, our trust's corporate plan was clearly being buffeted by external factors which are being obscured by political considerations. How the relatively short-term future will unfold is unknown. In the context of the NHS, HR planning is clearly a dynamic process. There will never be an ideal distribution of hospitals agreed by all. Political considerations will ensure that centrally determined objectives will change, and that these will never present a clear planning framework for the trust. Trust managers need to attempt to anticipate the decisions of politicians.

In the short run the trust based its human resource requirements on previous experience and the currently expressed intentions of the purchasers. Its staffing estimates have been adjusted in line with anticipated funding from these purchasers, the anticipated funding forming the budget. Some reorganisation of production via the use of work study provided economies in the existing use of staff. Again, Chapter 9 shows that the corporate strategy, and hence the HRM strategy, very quickly became outdated.

# 2

# The HRM Debate

The authors' position on this debate is clearly stated in the introduction. This debate is so widely conducted that its detail cannot be ignored. A purpose of this chapter is to identify the main issues and to try to provide some kind of context for future discussion of our trust. Anybody coming new to the subject of HRM might be excused for believing that HRM is the 'science of lists'. The usual starting-point is a list of features of what is said to characterise personnel management, contrasted with a list of what characterises HRM. As suggested in the introduction, it is equally possible to place approximate dates – for example, pre-1980s, post-1980s – and under both dates list a set of management practices as characterising the two eras.

As Brian Towers succintly states in his foreword to Oliver and Wilkinson (1992:xi), 'Something started to go wrong with the British economy soon after the Great Exhibition of 1851.' He goes on to point out that America, a post-war example for 'The Great and the good', to visit and emulate in terms of business practice and management, now could be in long-term decline and that the 'German economic miracle' looks less attractive than it once appeared. At the time of writing, Towers' was pointing to the 'stunning' performance of Japan over the previous 20 years. Japan had become a source of emulation, but primarily in terms of current management practices, as opposed to macroeconomic and political and social policies.

This latter point cannot be ignored in identifying the source of such practices in the UK, many of which have become associated with HRM. Japan is currently suffering economic and competitive difficulties. These are affecting their so-called 'leading-edge' companies associated with the management practices referred to. According to Wickens (1994), most of the 'benevolent' employment practices associated with Japan applied to only 20 per cent of the labour force. Many workers, especially women, were in insecure, peripheral, employment.

**Objective Circumstances**

Following Towers, something started to go wrong with the world economy during the 1970s. A long-term economic recession, unevenly distributed, began and has continued into the 1990s. For the advanced economies this was exacerbated by increased competitiveness from the Pacific Basin, and more recently by the competitive potential from the Eastern European countries. The USA and the UK partly responded with a combination of a reversal to free market economics and a drive to cut unit labour costs. Linked to this, and particularly relevant to our NHS focus, was the attempt to cut government expenditures as a proportion of GNP. Government expenditure was seen as imposing costs on industry via taxation, combined with the disincentive effects of such taxation on individuals. For a brief explanation of the theoretical rationale, see Burchill (1992:ch. 2). These forces are well recognised in the HRM literature. In terms of our debate on the meaning of HRM, Legge (1989:40) suggests that 'in many cases, the use of the 'new label' is no more or less than a reflection of the 'new right' at the place of work... Our new enterprise culture demands a new language, one that asserts management's right to manipulate.'

There is no doubt that in order to survive organisations need to be competitive. In terms of our concern with the NHS it has been stated that:

> The agenda for 1994 will be a substantial reduction in the number of independent trusts, the closure of hospitals, bed reduction and staff reduction for hospital-based trusts, and substantial reorganisations for community trusts. The private sector and professional self-employment are now active players in this scene, and the NHS has to be in shape to face the challenge.

The author concluded that six concerns faced the director of personnel at NHSE level; five of these were said to be 'productivity', with number six being 'reward for greater productivity'. *Health Service Journal* (10 February 1994).

Whether or not the above constitutes the position of the NHS is beside the point. The theme is a common one, and a slogan widely used in the NHS is 'More for Less'. What is implied is the need for widespread reform of 'production' methods and the use of labour. Making labour work more intensively – 'work harder' – is one way of improving productivity. Another is to make labour work more efficiently – 'work smarter'. Either could result in labour being rewarded with higher pay, and both or either could result in lower unit labour costs. Wickens (1994:31) quotes Sengenberger to the effect that there is a need to achieve a new 'synthesis between higher efficiency and higher quality of work and jobs'. This last conceptualisation adds a dimension. The ideal presumably is that the employment relationship becomes one which is transformed to produce more interesting and enjoyable jobs, resulting in higher quality products, greater volume of output and greater rewards for all participants. A further dimension is usually added. This state of affairs is not imposed by those 'who know better': it is secured via involvement and participation by all concerned.

Storey and Sisson (1993:235) point to the need for another kind of 'synthesis': 'The time to seek out the appropriate balance between individualism and collectivism has now arrived.' If we combine this desire for 'syntheses' (and there are others – 'the best of British and the best of Japanese', 'control and motivation' (Wickens, 1994)) we have a prescription of Utopian grandeur: highly productive workers, producing high quality goods, in a benevolent and secure working environment, within a society which gets the best from both individual potential and collective action. There appears also to be a 'synthesis' of the views of academics and practioners on a prescriptive level. A problem has been identified to which there is a solution. We could be approaching the end of history.

There are critics. Part of the criticism has been implied above. Many current management practices could be associated with the consequences of a recession, and increased competition, for the labour force. Where labour is weak it can be made to work harder and its collaboration is more easily secured. In this model, current management practices are a combination of updated

'Taylorism' and its ideology of competition, and a recasting of 'human relations' techniques and their ideology of collaboration. What we see is increased exploitation of the labour force by a combination of coercion via the market and new technology, and a use of manipulative techniques derived from the field of human relations.

It could be argued that the above contains a melange of HRM, total quality management (TQM), lean production and so on, and that these are distinct components of management practice. In reality it is difficult to disentangle these. These are concepts which will be explored in more detail later. Suffice to say that Bowen and Lawler (1992) discuss the impact of TQM on HRM and could really be discussing the differences between personnel management and HRM. For example, TQM requires single status approaches, flexibility, greater training, teamworking and the rest. This fits with the approach that current management practices simply require a different pattern of behaviour within the traditional areas of personnel management, rather than the notion that a distinct field of study, HRM, has emerged. Before pursuing this argument further, some attempt needs to be made to identify the ingredients of Taylorism and human relations and their constituent ideologies.

**Taylorism**

Frederick Winslow Taylor (1856–1915) published a book in 1911 called *The Principles of Scientific Management*. The terms *Taylorism* and *scientific management* have become almost synonymous. The definition of *work study* given on p. 13 could have come from Taylor's work. This aspect of Taylorism has been the most influential part of his model – influential in the sense of being widely utilised by employers.

Taylor believed that there was one best way of performing any task and that this could be discovered by the use of scientific methods. This 'best' way would produce the greatest quantity of output in a given period of time at least cost to the employee in terms of effort. Tasks themselves needed to be properly identified in terms of their contribution to the final product. Examining the whole production process might lead to a redesign of tasks, or work, the generation of new tasks and the removal of others on the grounds of efficiency. The time allowed to perform tasks could be identified by measuring the performance of 'ideal' workers. The above represents a combination of method study and time study.

Built into Taylor's approach was the belief that specialisation of labour would be more effective than flexibility. It also led to workers concentrating on very simple, repetitive tasks. Taylor saw the work study process, and therefore all the planning of work, as belonging to management. Workers might be capable of such planning, but they had neither the time, money nor perspective to do this scientifically. Management becomes a bureaucratic process based on expertise. Looked at from the workers' point of view, such a development would render their earlier developed skills redundant and make their labour less valuable in the market for it. It would also make their work less interesting. Managers would be taking the knowledge of the workers away from them and using it to their detriment. At the same time, managers would be securing more control over the workforce.

Taylor also believed in a 'fair day's pay for a fair day's work.' Scientifically determining the time allowed for a task would ultimately determine 'a fair day's work', in Taylor's model. That this is a problematic relationship requires no further discussion. 'A fair day's pay' was less amenable to determination by such a simple formula. What did emerge was the view that pay should be closely related to output. The main ingredients of Taylorism were detailed analysis of work, specialisation, bureaucratic control by trained managers, with the separation of planning from doing, and a theory of motivation based on economic rewards. It could be interpreted as a system designed to ensure maximum exploitation of labour. (See Braverman, 1974, for a detailed critique of this approach.) We will see that there were earlier criticisms of Taylorism, some of which will be discussed under the section on human relations (see below). A question central to this chapter is whether or not we have a revival of Taylorism within the HRM/TQM/lean production approaches to managing labour. Rose (1988:36) says of Taylor's world-view, 'It is discredited today because of our distrust for all technocrats but could well revive if economic trouble continues.'

There are controversies relating to what precisely Taylorism or scientific management consists of. These are explored in Rose (1988) and Braverman (1974). For the purpose of this text its important dimension is the examination and reorganisation of the work process to secure increased productivity, with the main focus being on method and time study. In this process labour is essentially a measurable entity with identifiable physical and mental abilities which can be manipulated by management to fit the technological requirements of production. The amount of effort that can be extracted from labour is a function of rewards and punishments, and clearly identifiable notions of fatigue and its causes. Where labour has autonomy, it will use this to minimise its efforts to secure the rewards on offer. A role of management is to prevent labour from circumventing its attempts to achieve optimum use of all resources.

The above represents the mainstream characterisation of Taylorism. Taylor was not oblivious to human relations issues, and did believe that the collaboration of labour was necessary. He also believed that, where his methods were 'properly' intoduced, the outcomes for labour were so positive that its collaboration was inevitable. A constant message behind all prescriptive managerial approaches, whether Taylor or human relations-based, or both, is that problems only arise because of a failure to introduce proposed systems properly.

## Human Relations

The term 'Human Relations' is used here in a way which is specific to this text. Its use is designed to highlight developments in management thought which were not, and are not, included in the kind of depiction of Taylorism given above, and elsewhere. Historically, the Hawthorne Investigations of 1927–32 are said to have been critical in the development of what came to be called the Human Relations School. (See Rose, 1988, for a more detailed account.)

Human relations is associated with the idea that workers are not simply atomistic individuals who can be slotted into technological and bureaucratic systems. They have, and develop, social and group relationships both at and outside the place of work and they bring to the place of work specific and varied characteristics. Also the notion of their motivation, and relationship to work being linked solely to monetary reward and punishment, is seen to be wrong.

Implicit in the above is a criticism of Taylorism. It is not always possible to carefully select the right type of worker for the job and slot that worker into a predetermined system. The place of work is a social system with all its attributes. Its survival depends on the commitment and involvement of those within it. Motivation requires recognition and status. It is a simple step from the above to the rhetoric of empowerment, teamworking and so on (see below). The conclusions derived from the Hawthorne Investigations gave scope for social psychologists and sociologists to display their wares at the place of work. Theories of motivation, group dynamics, leadership, organisational change and strategic management have developed. These are not all traditionally linked to human relations. The intention here is to distinguish between the ingredients of scientific management, as outlined above, and those approaches to HRM which place emphasis on the psychological and social role of the worker at the place of work, and how this can be manipulated without constant reference to coercion. This latter emphasis is being referred to as a human relations approach.

It is possible to argue that both approaches have always been used but with the emphasis on one or the other shifting. Braverman (1974:145) tells us:

> The 'human relations' approach, first of a series of behavioral sociological schools, focused on personnel counseling and on ingratiating or nonirritating styles of 'face to face' supervision. But these schools have yielded little to management in the way of solid and tangible results. Moreover, the birth of the 'human relations' idea coincided with the Depression of the 1930s and the massive wave of working-class revolt that culminated in the unionization of the basic industries of the United States. In the illumination cast by these events, the workplace suddenly appeared not as a system of bureaucratic formal organisation on the Weberian model, nor as a system of informal group relations as in the interpretation of Mayo and his followers, but rather as a system of power, of class antagonisms. Industrial psychology and sociology have never recovered from this blow. From their confident beginnings as 'sciences' devoted to discovering the springs of human behavior the better to manipulate them in the interests of management, they have broken up into a welter of confused and confusing approaches pursuing psychological, sociological, economic, mathe-

matical, or 'systems' interpretations of the realities of the workplace, with little real impact upon the management of worker or work.

Braverman is quoted at length becauses he touches on a recurrent cycle of thought amongst academics. Fox (1966:3–4) quotes the then chairman of the CBI:

> In my company, such expressions as 'Team Spirit', 'Team Work', and 'Working Together' are commonly used... It is my belief that they are more than catch phrases; *they are important and meaningful expressions of a concept which underlies the activities of our business* [Fox's italics]. The whole view of industrial organisation embodied in this unitary emphasis has long since been abandoned by *most social scientists as incongruent with reality and useless for purposes of analysis* [our italics].

Gold (1993:1) tells us:

> Over the years, innumerable studies have attempted to come to grips with solutions to these problems. One of the most enduring, developed from the 1920s onwards, has been the introduction of groupwork – the replacement of Taylorite-style production systems by groups of employees working in teams. The worker should not, it is claimed, be seen as an isolated individual left to confront production technology alone, but as a member of a team which plans, produces and monitors as a joint exercise. Such a view not only meets the workers' social needs but also, according to the argument, promotes efficiency and quality. This perspective, *which remained for many years the preserve mainly of academics and theorists* [our italics] has now become more widely accepted and advocated for a variety of reasons...In these circumstances, teamwork is hardly a fad or luxury, but a necessity.

Fox (1966) goes on to advocate a pluralist approach at the place of work. Conflict and sectional interests have to be recognised and accommodated. Braverman sees the conflict as fundamental and something which is either suppressed or manipulated. This is sometimes described as a conflict approach. Gold advocates a unitarist approach: the 'them' and 'us' attitude can be broken down. (See Burchill, 1992:ch. 1, for more detail on these approaches.)

The three quotations above highlight some of the differences which exist amongst academics. In the UK, pluralism was accepted by management in the 1960s and 1970s as an approach. The 1980s and 1990s have seen greater emphasis on unitarism. Academics appear to have extolled the virtues of whichever approach appears to appeal to management, depending upon when they were writing. Management have found convenient rationalisations for their activities in such writing. This is, of course, a very broad generalisation. Not all academics have engaged in prescription. Nevertheless, the contradictions embodied in the three quotations tell us a great deal about the opportunistic and speculative nature of much academic writing.

## Human Resource Management

Storey (1992:ch. 2) provides an excellent account of the different interpretations given to the concept of HRM. The first of these is that it basically replaces the term 'personnel management'. An alternative is that the traditional areas and techniques of personnel management are brought together in a more integrated fashion. This second interpretation could be carried further so that the human resource is seen as equivalent to other resources such as capital, land and so on, to be manipulated in pursuit of an integrated business plan and strategy. Storey goes on to suggest that none of these approaches contains any new or distinctive element and that they are all compatible with a range of widely differing characteristics. On page 25 he writes:

> if the HRM appellation is to apply there needs to be some extra qualifying factor such as an underlying logic in pursuit of employee 'commitment' or some similar characteristic feature...Associated with this 'stronger' version of HRM is the idea that there is a philosophical underpinning to it which sharply marks it off from Taylorism and indeed from the pluralistic conventions of industrial relations orthodoxy.

The analysis allows for a distinction between what he calls the 'hard' and 'soft' versions of HRM. In the hard version the human resource is as manipulable and disposable as other factors of production. In the soft version the emphasis is on the specific human contribution which gives this factor a unique value, often embodied in the slogan 'our people are our most valued asset'. The definitions of HRM can be characterised as ranging from 'weak' – same as personnel management – to 'strong' – distinctive. Guest

(1989) writes in terms of 'loose' and 'tight' definitions of HRM, as opposed to Storey's 'weak' and 'strong'.

Storey (1992) goes on to elaborate the components of the strong version. He stresses the importance of the human resource as 'making the difference' and its need to be 'nurtured'. The quantity and quality of the human resource are issues for top management which feed into rather than derive from the corporate plan. It follows from this that HRM is of integral concern to line managers and is not the sole possession of personnel managers. The traditional areas of personnel management are then described by Storey as being the 'key levers' used to 'activate the HRM approach'. He goes on to say:

> These relate to a systematic and integrated approach to managing certain critical events: the inflow into the organisation; the clear communication of objectives; the calculated deployment of the human resource; the evaluating of its performance and the rewarding of it accordingly. The tools are to be used to seek not merely compliance but commitment (pp. 27–8).

There appears to be general acceptance that the approach is individualist/unitarist rather than collectivist/pluralist. A point made by Guest (1989) is that to show that HRM is distinctive 'requires a theory of HRM which is tightly defined but which embraces both the 'soft' and 'hard' components'. This point is not made explicitly by Storey. What it suggests is that the hard and soft versions of HRM are not alternatives – the word 'component' implies that both are aspects of HRM in practice. This last point is meant to imply that the 'hard'/'soft' dichotomy is a misleading one. The argument in this text is that 'hard' is a variant on Taylorism, and 'soft' a variant on human relations approaches. They work together and do not offer alternative approaches or versions. They are rhetorical devices. For example, the 'hard' rhetoric may be more useful in persuading senior managers at strategic decision making levels, with the 'soft' being part of the process of manipulating the workforce. The 'soft' rhetoric is also more reassuring to managers seeking to justify their policies to themselves. Our conclusion is that current management practice does not have a 'philosophical underpinning which sharply marks it off fom Taylorism'. In fact, we would see it as sharply linked to Taylorism.

*What, then, is HRM?*

Storey produces a list of 27 points of difference between what he calls 'personnel and IR' and 'HRM' Storey (1992:35). This kind of analysis could be described as 'comparative static': two notionally 'ideal' types of management are listed according to characteristics, in a 'before' and 'after' sense. Almost by implication, 'after' is in some way superior to 'before'. The types are not linked by historical or dynamic analysis. HRM is not being identified in the literature as a field of academic study – such as economics, sociology or, for that matter, industrial relations. The point being made here is that, from the academic point of view, HRM is not a new methodology and it does not denote a new area of study.

An alternative approach to the meaning of HRM is that in the 'management of people in work organisations' Sisson (1989:3) there has been a qualitative change in recent years. This is so substantial a change that it warrants the new title, HRM. Sisson tells us:

> The term personnel management is used here to describe the policies, processes and procedures involved in the management of people in work organisations. As will be seen from the book's list of contents, the term covers the design of organisations, as well as planning, recruitment and selection,appraisal training and development, remuneration, discipline, and participation and involvement.

The list of contents referred to by Sisson would certainly fit most texts on HRM. This applies not only to those texts which have been reissued as texts on HRM which previously described themselves as texts on personnel management, but to the literature in general. What we are left with is the question posed above: are the changes in the area of personnel management so substantial in qualitative terms that where these are practised we are into a completely new era of the management of human resources and the nature of the employment relationship?

If we think back to Taylor, we are told by Braverman (1974:87): 'The successors to Taylor are to be found in engineering and work design, and in top management' – a point of some significance. Taylor's activities and theories had clear implications for practice in the field of the management of human resources. A good deal of what is currently associated with HRM, or personnel management, is being driven by Taylor's successors, the work design engineers and top management. Under competitive pressure, and in a spirit of emulation, companies are introducing wide-ranging programmes of change which affect personnel departments. These programmes are predominantly Taylorite in conception.

Under the heading of 'Manufacturing Methods', Oliver and Wilkinson (1992) include such things as total quality control, more usually described as total quality management (TQM), quality circles, just in time (JIT) and so on. Reference is also made to lean production. Trade unions in the UK have tended to treat many of these terms as synonymous with HRM. For example, the GMB (1994) say: 'HRM developed in the 1980s and one problem we face in dealing with it is that as a doctrine it has many names. For example: Total Quality Management, Employee Involvement, Japanese Production Management, Lean Production.' The point being made here is that top management in many companies have sought to achieve organisational and behavioural changes to accommodate wide-ranging changes in production methods, with consequent changes in work design. Although not originating from personnel departments, such changes have an impact on personnel management practices. Much of what is used to define HRM is built into these change programmes introduced under such headings as TQM, lean production and JIT. Sometimes the literature separates these programmes from HRM, sometimes, as indicated, they become inextricably linked.

The problem is further complicated by the fact that each of these concepts overlaps. TQM incorporates JIT, lean production incorporates TQM, and therefore JIT. Often the whole thing is referred to as 'Japanese production methods', or even 'Japanisation'. The more the literature is examined, the more elusive the concept of HRM. Lucio and Weston (1992:215) in an examination of trade union responses to HRM talk about 'strategies commonly placed under the heading of HRM', without attempting a definition of HRM. This could be a way forward.

This text is going to rely on an examination of the role of a personnel department, in a situation of considerable organisational change, and attempt to relate what happens there to the range of practices and approaches referred to in this chapter. For example, the account of human resource planning given in Chapter 1 could be considered in terms of the concept of strategy, linking policy to environmental change and the relevance of the corporate or business plan. Put in these terms, is what is happening sufficient to satisfy the requirement of HRM that it is strategic planning, and something more than the traditional pragmatic response of a personnel department?

The next section of this chapter will try to summarise the main ingredients of TQM, JIT and so on. It will be left to the reader to decide whether or not we simply have a combination of Taylorism and human relations, updated to take account of the possibilities of information technology and a large scale recession, rather than something more profound.

## Total Quality Management

The term 'TQM' is used more generally in the literature than the term 'total quality control' (TQC). Oliver and Wilkinson (1992), dealing with Japanisation, use the term 'TQC'. Dale and Cooper (1992:137), at the beginning of their chapter, 'The Japanese Approach to TQM', immediately switch to TQC, which they tell us (p. 138) 'readily translates into total quality care and total quality commitment'. This text will continue to use the term 'TQM'.

According to Dale and Cooper (1992:137), 'Most experts are agreed that quality is the dominant factor in the success of Japanese companies in world markets.' The experts may or may not be correct, but what is certain is that the word 'quality' is now very widely used by all organisations. TQM is seen as much more than simply emphasising and achieving quality: it is seen as a process which permeates all aspects of the organisation of production. A cryptic definition is given in Marchington (1992:32): 'a systematic process of management in which all employees are expected to see others, both internal and external to the organisation, as customers for their services'. This is a definition which manages not to use the word 'quality'.

As with most of these concepts, and as we have seen with HRM, it is possible to identify TQM by reference to lists of features and requirements. The main advantage of such a list is not that it presents us with some kind of ideal – a rationalisation used by Storey to justify his HRM list – but that it enables the reader to identify terminology currently in vogue and thus give some kind of meaning to it. TQM, like most management conceptualisations, promises quality, efficiency, participation, and happiness and well-being for all concerned. If any of these outcomes appear not to follow from the process, then it is obvious that TQM is not being properly applied. This was an argument widely used by Taylor: if anything went wrong where Taylorism was said to be applied, it must have been applied incorrectly.

The process contains many sub-processes and the reader will be comforted to know that these can be divided into 'hard' and 'soft'. Marchington (1992:93) neatly summarises this:

> The British Quality Associaton (BQA) has put forward three defini-
> tions of TQM. The first focuses on the so-called 'soft', qualitative char-
> acteristics, found elsewhere in the work of US consultants such as
> Tom Peters: customer orientation, culture of excellence, removal of
> performance barriers, teamwork, training, employee participation,
> competitive edge. From this perspective, TQM is seen as consistent
> with open management styles, delegated responsibility and increased
> autonomy to staff. The second definition places emphasis on the pro-
> duction aspects such as systematic measurement and control of work,
> setting standards of performance, using statistical procedures to assess
> quality; this is the 'hard' production or operations management type
> view, which arguably leads to less discretion for employees. The third
> definition comprises three features: an obsession with quality, the
> need for a scientific approach, and all in one turn, thus borrowing
> from the above definitions albeit in a unitarist fashion.

The above quotation contains a list of features of TQM, a list which can easily be expanded. Furthermore, as one develops the discussion of the concept, it begins to overlap a range of issues. Many of the ingredients of HRM, as earlier indicated, overlap TQM. Often both are associated with significant organisational change related to market pressures. One way forward is to identify the components of a company strategy involved in large-scale change and reorganisation.

*Land Rover*

According to Dale and Cooper (1992:20), 'Without the total commitment of the CEO and his or her immediate executives and other senior managers, nothing much will happen and anything that does will not be permanent. They must take personal charge and exercise forceful and personal leadership'. The implementation of TQM is a top-down process. For Rover the first stage was a consultant-led training of senior management in the meaning and full implications of total quality improvement (TQI). According to Rover, TQI has seven main ingredients:

| | |
|---|---|
| The philosophy | prevention not detection |
| The approach | management-led |
| The scale | everyone responsible |
| The measure | the costs of quality |
| The standard | right first time |
| The scope | company-wide |
| The theme | continuous improvement |

The last of these, continuous improvement – often referred to by its Japanese translation, *kaisen* – is the most important of the above. It underpins the notion of TQI as a process which continues indefinitely. There is no limit to improvement within this concept, based on the belief that nothing is ever perfect. However, improvement always relates to cost minimisation and productivity growth. Kaisen puts an onus on all employees to constantly seek out improvement.

The literature and practitioners identify different types of groups concerned with improvement to which the term 'quality' is attached. Before examining these groups, the word 'quality' itself needs some consideration. In many respects the TQM practitioners have reworked the term to give it a meaning equivalent to the terms *goods* and *services* in economic theory. Consumers demand goods and services to satisfy their needs. Producers respond by providing these. At any particular time what is produced will be designed to specifications reflective of consumer demands as identified by the producer. The extent to which individual consumer demands can be met depends upon the nature of the good or service and the associated production technology.

When purchasing a car the consumer generally has a choice of combinations of specifications. None of these choices might meet the specific demands of an individual consumer. However, standardisation allows cost reductions and consumers compromise on price. Producers need to understand the nature of this compromise and recognise the extent to which consumers are willing to pay for additional choice. Mass production techniques allow for large scale production of identical units of output at low cost. In late 1993, the Defender, the remodelled Land Rover, was being produced at the rate of 480 per week (Casey:1993). There is a basic design and it follows that to mean anything in comparative terms, these Defenders would be *homogeneous* products – they would be identical. When economists talk about the demand for a product they have in mind this notion of homogeneity. Quality would mean achieving the output of a product to meet the specifications contained in this notion of homogeneity: being identical. If a unit did not meet the specifications laid down for it by Rover, it would not be a Defender. Such a failure, if passed on to the consumer, would not meet the consumers' requirements, since these would be derived from the producer's specifications.

That the price relative to the product is of importance to the consumer is implied in the above. A defective, or below expected quality, product imposes costs on the consumer. An objective must be to ensure that this does not happen – the goodwill of the consumer is the future. Quality control involves additional costs which will feed back into price. Obviously the profit-maximising producer will aim to minimise all costs, a point we will come back to. A question addressed by the organisation of quality groups is how to minimise the cost of quality control, by which we mean ensuring that units of output always reach specifications.

One of the seven principles adopted by Rover, referred to above, is 'right first time'. Employees, referred to as 'associates' by the company, are encouraged to avoid, identify and notify defects and not simply pass them on. This is reinforced by the principle 'everyone responsible'. Associates are exhorted to take responsibility for the quality of their work and its improvement. One of the authors, in the 1970s, was involved in a dispute at Rover which concerned the grading of inspectors. Their job was to inspect components and finished vehicles for defects and to ensure that they were put right. In the current situation each associate is responsible for avoiding and identifying defects – the role of inspector no longer exists. The principle of 'prevention not detection' leads to the concept of quality teams. Dale and

Cooper (1992) identify a number of these. *Quality circles* are groups of six to eight people working in the same area of production. They meet voluntarily, facilitated by management, and try to identify areas for improvement and develop projects to improve production and solve problems. Proposals are presented to management and considered in terms of their feasability and cost effectiveness. *Quality project teams* are led by senior management, who identify objectives, and they consist of representatives of a range of organisational functions. The need for change could have been identified at any level within the organisation and the change is of a strategic nature. *Quality improvement teams* are set up to deal with non-strategic production problems usually identified below management levels. They are agreed with management but are led by below management level employees.

The latter two types of team are generally developed beyond one work area and are attempting to solve problems which have already been identified. Rover introduced what they called 'quality action teams' (QATs) and produced a 47 page booklet for their guidance. The purpose of a QAT is to convene 'to improve a given process by use of a systematic approach to problem solving'. The 'sponsoring group' of a QAT 'should ideally have sufficient authority to action any changes which the QAT demonstrates the worth of implementing.' The booklet goes on to outline modus operandi for such groups and to outline problem-solving techniques. There is no space here to elaborate in more detail. QATs are clearly related to the notion of kaisen, of prevention, and of employee involvement in getting it right first time.

What we have said so far about TQM illustrates its nature. It is linked to organisational and 'cultural' change on a big scale. Improving the competitive position of the organisation is a major objective. As suggested above, the change is top-down-initiated but generally provoked by competitive and turbulent market conditions. Not surprisingly TQM and HRM have become closely linked. The introduction of TQM can be associated with the notions of strategy linked to HRM and its defining characteristics are such that it has implications for personnel management. It is unitarist in perspective, emphasing organisation-wide responsibility for success, usually accompanied by a mission statement (Rover mission: 'To be internationally renowned for extra-

ordinary customer satisfaction') and places emphasis on communications and 'transformational leadership'. It is also business
and customer-oriented.

Changes at Rover incorporated radical change in the management structure. Six levels of hierarchy were reduced to three:
Senior manager, manager and associate: Management was 'delay-
ered'. All employees were given broader work roles with training
for flexibility. According to the Rover New Deal, Land Rover,
1992: 'Rover will be a single status Company.' This was defined to
include the abolition of clocking; a single status sick pay scheme;
free health checks; everybody wearing 'workwear'; single catering.

## Lean Production

According to Casey (1993) the 'principles of Rover Tomorrow –
The New Deal are based on the notion of "Lean Production"'.
Womack *et al.* (1990:13) tell us:

> Lean production (a term coined by IMVP researcher John Krafcik) is
> 'lean' because it uses less of everything compared with mass produc-
> tion – half the human effort in the factory, half the manufacturing
> space, half the investment in tools, half the engineering hours to
> develop a new product in half the time. Also, it requires keeping far
> less than half the needed inventory on site, results in far fewer defects,
> and produces a greater and ever growing variety of products.

For an interesting discussion of some of the terminology used in
this quotation, see Lyddon (1993). The distinction should be
between production methods which rely on large stocks of materials, capital, buildings, land and labour, and those which use less.
Mass production, as Wickens (1993) points out, can also be lean.
Lyddon reminds us that methods of production are usually classified into job, batch and flow. Mass is to do with quantity produced rather than the method of production and any method
could be used to produce in mass. We are referred by Lyddon to
Woollard (1954). What is demonstrated quite clearly by Lyddon
is that many of the 'principles of flow production' enunciated by
Woollard coincide with principles laid down by Womack *et al.*
(1990) and associated by him with Toyota. This is an extremely

important point. The rigorous imposition of a set of principles of production is as likely to relate to the context in which the attempt is made as it is to any absolute content these principles might have. Toyota have simply adopted a system of production incorporating principles of work design clearly enunciated by Woollard in 1954.

Lyddon (1993:33) reminds us of a point made by Woollard: 'Woollard made the salutary observation that flow production "like all tools of management...can be misused. ...with its obvious sequences and accurate timing, [it] could be the instrument of a slave-driving tyranny".'

*Just in Time (JIT)*

JIT is very much associated with lean production, although as a term it was widely used before the term 'lean production' was popularised via Womack (1990). According to Womack *et al.* (1990:62):

> Ohno developed a new way to coordinate the flow of parts within the supply system on a day-to-day basis, the famous just-in-time system, called *kanban* at Toyota. Ohno's idea was simply to convert a vast group of suppliers and parts plants into one large machine...by dictating that parts would only be produced at each previous step to supply the immediate demand of the next step.

Because this eliminated all inventories and meant that any failure could bring the whole system to a standstill, it was a difficult system to introduce and took all of 20 years to complete (according to Womack).

JIT is probably best treated like the economic concept of optimisation. Any local shopkeeper is aware of the need to balance stocks against potential purchases and that holding stock costs money. In this context, zero stocks is an absurd notion. The experienced shopkeeper will try to balance the cost of holding stocks against the potential loss of profit of being out of stock. Car manufacturers are both purchasers and suppliers – they have suppliers and customers. If retailers are customers, they may be persuaded to hold stocks. Similarly suppliers may be persuaded to hold stocks. If the producer pushes the costs of holding stocks onto the supplier or retailer, the costs of stock holding still remain within the chain of supply to the consumer. JIT is a reworking of the notion of optimisation of use of resources into apparently practical devices for achieving this. Eliminating idle resources, whether it be idle space, idle components or idle labour time, throughout the whole production process is an ideal. However it does not follow that zero stocks and total utilisation of resources is an optimum. Fluctuations in demand, labour shortages and the potential for industrial action would all suggest otherwise.

A committed or, for that matter, compliant labour force might remove one of the threats. Monopsonistic purchasing power might help to control suppliers, and monopolistic production the retailers. Proponents of lean production and JIT talk about collaboration along the supply chain, and the notion of purchasers nurturing the suppliers through long-term contracts. Womack *et al.* (1990:148) says, 'At the heart of lean supply lies a different system of establishing prices and jointly analysing costs'. Apparently target prices are set for the product and costs then worked back to make the price achievable. All suppliers share information and appropriate costing methods are used to ensure minimum costs. Costs are determined on a price minus basis, rather than prices on a cost plus basis. (Price minus costing versus cost plus pricing as the route to profit maximisation is a long-standing debate in the field of economics.)

This close relationship with suppliers helps the JIT process. In practice, what we seem to have is constant surveillance of areas where cost can be reduced. That waste should be eliminated is a tautology determined by the definition of waste. The problem in practice is identifying what exactly constitutes waste, and the extent to which others can be made to bear costs as a result of discrepancies in market power. Suppliers are set cost targets by essentially monopsonistic purchasers. Labour is expected to be more flexible to reduce idle time, thus intensifying effort. Nevertheless the message of Womack *et al.* is that everybody benefits from and is happier under lean production.

This chapter has attempted to give background and meaning to the debate on HRM. It has also illustrated how idealisations of HRM overlap with idealisations of TQM, JIT and lean production. It is not surprising that the terms tend to be used interchangeably. Future topics will be related back to the present and the first chapter, and some of the concepts associated with these topics but not discussed here will be picked up later.

In terms of our focus on the NHS, NHS managers attend courses which contain inputs from car industry managers emphasising the merits of lean production and the need to re-engineer the workforce. It is important to remember that the NHS contains production units which are not driven by a track, producing homogeneous and measurable units of output. Hospitals, for example, work seven-day 24-hour systems, without shutdowns for maintenance or other purposes. Managers supervise a complex range of staff, which cannot be reduced to operatives, ranging from people, and teams, with world-wide reputations – some staff earn more than their CEOs. They also have their 'customers' on the premises, day in, day out.

What follows from this is that the current management practices referred to above will take on a different form in the NHS. The purchaser/provider split will allow the purchasers, like car manufacturers, or large supermarket chains, to impose conditions on their suppliers – the providers. Taylorite methods will be used to secure work reorganisation, and human relations techniques to secure worker compliance. This process can be observed in operation without worrying about whether or not we use the term 'personnel management' or 'HRM' to examine the resourcing, staff development and employee relations activities of an organisation. HRM is used in this text because the authors believe that it will continue to replace 'personnel management' as the term used to indicate these sets of activities.

**Summary**

The term 'HRM' is used in this text as an alternative to 'personnel management'. Current management practices can easily be classified using traditional notions of scientific management and human relations. In the same way traditional critiques and analyses can be used to explore the impact of these practices. What is significant about the present situation is the pervasiveness of the rhetoric and practices, partly linked to the globalisation of companies and competition, and the output of business schools. These forces, combined with information technology, do generate qualitative differences in the impact of a long-term depression on work design and organisation from those experienced in earlier phases of the trade cycle.

What is not apparent, also, is that a new methodology, subject area or approach has emerged that makes more sense of what is going on than those associated with labour process analysis. This text will attempt to examine how these pressures manifest themselves in a NHS setting.

# 3

# Industrial Relations in the NHS

The most comprehensive survey of industrial relations in the NHS is to be found in Seifert (1992). This chapter is concerned with providing a brief outline of the system as it currently operates and identifying some of the forces for change. It also examines trade unions in the NHS.

## Whitleyism

The First World War was preceded by considerable industrial unrest and conflict. According to Phelps Brown (1986:142), 'the war years 1914–18 mark the rapid development of industrial relations at the place of work under the stimulus of full employment. …The unrest in industry had risen to a menacing pitch in 1917.' In 1916, Asquith set up the Reconstruction Committee of which the Whitley Committee was a sub-committee. J. C. Whitley, Deputy Speaker of the House, chaired the sub-committee which produced five reports between 1917 and 1919. The committee's terms of reference were to suggest ways of securing permanent improvements in the relations between employers and workmen, and to recommend that those directly concerned systematically reviewed these relations to maintain improvements. The committee was asked to examine the whole of industry and not just the public sector. This is not the place to relate the history of the implementation of these recommendations, or to examine their precise content. Suffice to say that the negotiating arrangements established in parts of the public sector in the period following the Second World War are referred to as 'Whitley Arrangements'. These were applied to the NHS.

For our purposes Whitleyism is defined as a system which has several dimensions:

1. that pay and terms and conditions of employment are best determined at national level by strong employers negotiating with strong trade unions;
2. that such agreements should be supported by procedures – on disciplinary and grievance matters, for example – that are nationally based;
3. at the place of work there should be provision and support for joint consultation;
4. implicit in the above is a belief in collective bargaining and the principle of trade union recognition.

In the decades following the inception of the NHS a system representing the above developed. When McCarthy produced his review of Whitley in 1976 he told us:

> The constitution of the Whitley Councils of the Health Service provides at present for eleven Whitley Councils, a General Council and ten functional Whitley Councils, viz:
>
> Administrative and Clerical Staffs
> Ancillary Staffs
> Ambulancemen
> Dental (Local Authorities)
> Medical and (Hospital) Dental
> Nurses and Midwives
> Optical
> Pharmaceutical
> Professional and Technical 'A'
> Professional and Technical 'B' (McCarthy, 1976)

In 1963, the pay of the dental and medical councils was placed under a system based on recommendations of a doctors and dentists review body to the prime minister, and the two functional councils ceased to meet. This, then, represented the evolution of Whitley in the NHS to 1976.

A major dispute over pay in 1982 led to the setting up in 1983 of a review body for nursing staff, midwives, health visitors and professions allied to medicine. This also reports directly to the prime minister. At the same time it was decided that general managers' pay would be directly determined by the secretary of state. Since then, performance-related pay (PRP) has been introduced for general and senior managers.

The way the system is supposed to work is that the General Whitley Council (GWC) lays down general conditions and procedures which apply to all employees, and the functional councils and review bodies deal with matters specific to the groups covered. For example, the GWC deals with such things as holiday entitlements, removal and travel expenses, redundancy and sick pay provisions; the functional councils and review bodies are mainly concerned with the pay of their constituent groups. Each Whitley Council is made up of management and staff side representatives. Notionally they negotiate agreements which are recommended to the secretary of state. The review bodies consist of panels appointed through the Office of Manpower Economics. Management and unions give evidence to these bodies who then make recommendations to the prime minister.

If the above accurately represented the situation as it currently exists then it would be possible to argue that the Whitley dimensions referred to earlier still remain relatively intact. A highly centralised system of pay determination supported by strong trade unions with some modification of the collective bargaining relationship appears to be in place. Mediation, via review bodies, is easily incorporated into any collective bargaining model. However, the existence of trusts complicates the picture, as does the acceptance by the government of the PRB recommendations of 1995, and the 'enabling agreement' reached at Whitley in 1994.

Trusts are free to negotiate their own terms and conditions of employment for all staff – with the exception of junior doctors. Staff transferred to trusts are entitled to carry existing contracts with them, but these can be dealt with by persuasion or giving appropriate notice in accordance with such contracts. Given that neither Whitley nor the review bodies had been giving very much in terms of increased benefits, within a framework of cash limits supported by staff reductions and unemployment, there had been, for the 1990s, little need for trust managers to be adventurous, or overtly confrontational. However there is plenty of evidence that regulation was being devolved, even if collective bargaining was not. New employees were taken on with new contracts and there were widespread changes in shift patterns, grade mixes and work intensity, all being imposed at trust level. Emerging patterns of bargaining and regulation will be discussed below.

According to Glascott (1994:12), 'A recent survey by the NHS Trust Federation showed overwhelming support for the dismantling of Whitley (95%) and the review bodies (92.2%).' This, of course, represents the views of trust management. The same publication proposed that both Whitley and the pay review bodies should be rapidly phased out. In late 1994 and early 1995 moves were made in the direction of achieving both these objectives. In 1994 non-review body staff agreed a settlement with a provision enabling local pay. The 1995 PRB recommendations, for nurses, midwives, health visitors and professions allied to medicine were that there should be a 1 per cent increase in national pay supplemented by local negotiations. The NHSE advised purchasers that in most cases this would produce total increases of between 1.5 per cent and 3 per cent for most staff in these categories. Purchasers were reminded that the PRB had proposed no upper limit. The same letter, EL(95)34, announced that 'we can expect over 93 per cent of NHS staff to receive pay increases at least partially determined locally'. Both national and-local agreements were to take effect from 1 April 1995.

Doctors and dentists were granted a national pay increase of 2.5 per cent. EL(95)34 saw this as meaning that 'progress on local pay' would be slower for these groups. However no upper limit was set to the increases which could be offered to consultants at local level, although the average increase for consultants was limited to 5 per cent at trust level. The PRB recommendations, accepted by the government, neatly fitted the government's overall objectives of developing autonomy at trust level. They also neatly divided doctors and nurses. An immediate reaction of the RCM was to secure from its membership a withdrawal of its 'no industrial action' policy. The RCN, feeling it had some special relationship with the government, sought a meeting with the prime minister, which was refused. UNISON and the professional unions embarked on a strategy of rejecting local bargaining in respect of nurses, midwives, health visitors and PAMs. UNISON was thus put in the odd position of supporting local pay in the

NHS for one group of its members, non-PRB staff, and opposing it for members who were PRB staff. In June 1995, the RCM reached an agreement with the NHSE which included their acceptance of local bargaining.

Trusts simply went ahead with local bargaining, dealing with a basically confused local membership. The year 1995 marks the total demise of the system described above as Whitleyism in the NHS. For further details of Whitley and the review bodies, the reader is again advised to refer to Seifert (1992). The above has been a bare outline which is meant to be sufficient to provide a framework against which change can be analysed. The NHS, and consequently its system of industrial relations, is on the edge of a precipice. In the next section trade unions in the NHS, especially the professional ones, will be examined. Industrial relations at the level of our trust will be discussed in the next chapter.

## Trade Unions in the NHS

Trade unions in the NHS fall roughly into two categories – professional unions and the general unions. The professional unions include such unions as the RCN, the BMA, the RCM and the CSP. General unions include such organisations as UNISON, MSF, GMB and TGWU. The professional unions operate specifically in the field of health care whilst the general unions have members across a whole range of industries. COHSE, until it recently became part of UNISON, was confined to health care, with the other constituents of UNISON, NUPE and NALGO, being basically public-sector unions. Although the RCN contains midwife and health visitor members, the professional unions tend to recruit from a single profession on an exclusive basis.

Because the NHS professional unions have such special characteristics, they are worthy of detailed and separate consideration in a text such as this. The general unions will be dealt with in passing.

### *Professional Unions*

These unions contain the larger proportion of membership. This membership is made up of professionally qualified practitioners.

Each profession is governed by a regulatory board. For example, the 1979 Nurses, Midwives and Health Visitors Act provided for their regulation by the United Kingdom Central Council(UKCC). Chiropodists, dietitians, medical laboratory scientific officers, occupational therapists, orthoptists, physiotherapists and radiographers are covered by the Council for the Professions Supplementary to Medicine (CPSM). Doctors have the General Medical Council (GMC) and dentists the General Dental Council (GDC).

These councils are required to maintain and update registers of those qualified to practise. They are also expected to determine the educational and training requirements of those eligible to be on the statutory registers, and to oversee conduct. Misconduct of a professional kind could result in a practitioner being struck of the register. Membership of these councils is partly made up of those elected by the registered practitioners and by government appointees. For example, the UKCC consists of 40 elected members and 20 appointed. The government has never conceded complete self regulation to the professions.

The Webbs (1897) produced an analysis of trade unions based on detailed case studies and empirical evidence. In this they identified what they called 'trade union methods and devices'. This was developed in Webbs (1917) and applied to what they referred to as 'professional associations'. The analysis can be applied currently to the professional unions in the NHS.

> Voluntary Associations of brain-workers use, though under other designations, the Method of Collective Bargaining, with its corollary of the Strike; the Method of Mutual Insurance, not only of a 'benevolent' kind, but also making much of 'Legal Benefit', and not altogether ignoring 'Victimisation Benefit'and 'Strike Benefit'; and the Method of Legal Enactment for obtaining improvements in professional status. (p. 46)

They also tell us that 'we find them adopting . . . a method peculiar to themselves ... the Statutory Register of Legally Authorised Practitioners' (Webb and Webb, 1917:p. 46).

The major distinction that the Webbs identified between these professional unions and other unions was that they relied more heavily on legal enactment than did other unions. Their main militancy was channelled into political influence to secure legislative rights and protection. This process is particularly recognised in the statutory register. While it can be argued that the register protects the public by guaranteeing standards, there is no doubt that it also generates exclusiveness by requiring qualifications in order to practise. We find that the governance of these organisations reflects their history as political pressure groups. They all tend to have education and professional departments, along with industrial relations departments. Education departments are used to provide the research to lobby for entrance requirements. The professional departments try to establish such things as staffing norms and skill mix. They also pursue professional standards and conduct and defence of members before the councils – such as the UKCC and the GMC. Industrial relations departments are concerned with pay and terms and conditions, general disciplinary matters and grievances.

In practice the functions of these departments overlap. Setting standards and codes of conduct can reinforce the exclusivity, and thus the bargaining power of these organisations. Codes of conduct are laid down by the councils, and these have the backing of statute. General managers, with line authority over clinicians, might find that clinicians fall back on specialist knowledge and such codes to prevent the managers securing their objectives. In Taylorite terms, securing control over clinicians becomes a formidable task for managers. This theme needs further development.

*NHS Reforms and the Professional Unions.* In Chapter 1 it was noted that the NHS was vulnerable to economic forces. The 1970s were as much a watershed in the NHS as elsewhere, particularly in terms of the effects of the depression continuing from that period. Cost saving and efficient use of resources became priorities. Because of the nature and scale of health care, and the underlying principles of its provision since 1948, challenges were made to all facets of its activities.

Since 1948, the main provider, the NHS, had operated on basically socialist lines. Care was provided free at the point of delivery. This raised the question of how much care could be provided: to what level of need should people be treated? Even if the basis of care provision and its level were agreed this still raised the question of efficiency. All three aspects came to be questioned in the 1970s. The 1974 reforms aimed to integrate a service fragmented between local authority and central government, and to generate greater control over the providers' use of resources. Accountability was strengthened, but there was some devolution of management responsibility to district management teams and community health councils.

Management teams consisted of local representatives of medical and nursing staff operating on a consensus basis. Full integration was not achieved, and the developing economic crisis led to greater Treasury control and the imposition of cash limits. The 1979 Conservative government brought to bear an approach which began to question the principle of care delivered free and centrally funded. It also set in motion examinations of the total system, including whether or not it could be left entirely to the market place to provide health care. According to Lawson (1992:612–19) the government had to take account of the fact that health care was infinitely expandable. The system in the UK contained inefficiencies, but was at least as efficient and effective as systems operated in other countries. However it was believed that the provision of private health care should not be discouraged and that charges within the NHS could be increased substantially. Efficiency would be best improved by separating providers and purchasers.

Implicit in the analysis was the view that the traditional professionals, especially doctors and nurses, however noble their individual aspirations, had a blinkered and, ultimately self-interested notion of management and organisation. Effective choice, competition and autonomy were all seen as components of efficiency – especially autonomy from direct government interference. Reorganisation of the system of management was seen as a key step forward to allow for the achievement of the other objectives. Important targets for control were the medical profession, closely followed by that of nursing. Doctors were seen as individualistic and oblivious to financial constraints, and protected from being given management responsibility by their union. Nurses were seen as uneducated and subservient, with a consequent neglect of nursing science and research. With their inadequate nurse training they would inevitably be incapable of adequately managing nursing. Nurse training required improved clinical and management content.

The implementation of Griffiths (1983) marked the first major step towards reaching the objectives summarised above. Essentially Griffiths introduced the notion of the need for general management to co-ordinate functional management. Since Griffiths a process of general management has developed, but not completely according to the Griffiths model. For example, at national level there is still no clear separation between senior politicians and the NHSE. The notion of a board similar to that of the board of a nationalised industry, responsible for day-to-day management without ministerial interference, has not emerged. At the end of 1996, the Secretary of State imposed a 50 per cent cut in management costs on all units, regardless of individual circumstances. There is strong control from the centre by the politicians who have ensured that their programme of reforms is driven forward in detail and not just in general principle.

If we look closely at the trust structure outlined in Chapter 1, we do see the equivalent to a CEO with line authority over a collection of directorates. We also see the incorporation of medical and clinical staff into line management. There is a board with overall responsibility for a corporate plan. It is above the level of the trust that the model does not match stated aspirations. Freedoms to manage and in particular to control pay bills have not asserted themselves as widely as the rhetoric demands. Nevertheless we have noted the way in which pressures for change are still developing. An important subtext in the reforms contains the objectives associated with controlling and reorganising medical and clinical staff. Consultant contracts have become more tightly controlled with the introduction of job plans. Clinical directorates, usually directed by senior consultants, result in closer peer group challenges to consultant behaviour which threatens corporate plans. This is further reinforced by the Patient's Charter, and the possible loss of GP fundholder contracts within the new market. The power of consultants is also being challenged by plans to reduce their training period, and thus increase their supply.

Devolvement of budgets has tightened control over all staff. Some of the reforms desired for nursing and midwifery staff are working their way through Project 2000. Project 2000, started in 1989, provides for university-based training. Students receive bursaries and are not employees of directly managed units (DMUs) or trusts. Funding is provided from the NHS at regional level. Whilst performing practical training in trusts or DMUs students are regarded as supernumerary. Project 2000 has been accompanied by the introduction of a generic category of employee called 'health care assistants' (HCAs). These can be employed in any area of NHS employment, and outside Whitley terms and conditions. Part of the rationale for their employment was that they would replace the lost student input, and so far they have been predominantly employed in nursing and midwifery areas of work. They are encouraged to improve their training through the National Vocational Qualification (NVQ) system. A prediction would be that NHS funding of university training will be cut back and increasingly the costs will be borne by individuals. Distance learning packages from the providers of education could lead to the cost of academic training associated with NVQs being pushed onto the individuals. A net effect of all of this is that NHS units will cease to bear training costs and dispose of residential facilities for nurse and midwifery trainees.

To summarise, the changes designed to simulate the impact of market forces are linked to changes in control over the professionals. These are further linked to straightforward Taylorite attempts to alter the design of work. Changes in the educational provision will make it easier to gain access to the professions. Project 2000 will provide a more elite and autonomous cadre of nurses and midwives with managerial skills and the capacity to take on tasks traditionally undertaken by doctors. The NHS priority of nurse prescribing is a step in this direction. Similarly, *Changing Childbirth* (1993) is designed to give midwives more autonomy from GPs and obstetricians. One can imagine a cascade of tasks downwards – from consultants and doctors to specialist nurses, from obstetricians and GPs to midwives, from nurses and midwives to HCAs. All of the above is combined with pressures to decentralise bargaining and work regulation.

*Professional Union Responses.* Earlier reference was made to the emphasis placed on legal enactment as a method by these organisations. In the period since the inception of the NHS it is possible to argue that pressures, particularly during the last 20 years, have forced these organisations to become more involved in the use of collective bargaining as a method. They were always represented on the Whitley Councils and therefore party to the centralised collective bargaining process. Because of their exclusivity, their independence from the TUC and the traditional conservatism of their membership, they have tended to be regarded by the general unions as not really quite capable of effective representation of members in the collective bargaining process. McCarthy (1976) tells us:

> Among staff organisations most discussion centred on the adequacy of professional associations in relation to collective bargaining. The trade unions took the view that while professional associations might be able to perform valuable functions for their members in areas such as the maintenance of professional standards, or training, they were not equipped to play an effective part in the area of collective bargaining.

For a period during the 1970s and 1980s TUC affiliates refused in some areas to 'sit down' with the professional unions in joint consultative committees. Since those days relationships between both sets of unions have become more co-operative as changes in the NHS have led them to identify common interests. Although, in terms of methods, the professional unions have always behaved as unions, the shift to collective bargaining has made their status as such more clearly recognisable.

A watershed period for the professional unions was clearly the 1970s. This period was marked by widespread industrial action which involved professional unions. See Seifert (1992:Ch. 6) for details. It was also a period in which legislation gave an impetus to the professional unions to acquire some of the formal apparel of trade unions. The 1971 Industrial Relations Act required registration as a trade union to secure immunities under that Act. A special register was established to allow for joint registration as companies, charities and trade unions. This register still exists and most of the unions under consideration are known as 'special register bodies'. Registration was further encouraged by time off provisions for the representatives of recognised independent trade unions to take part in trade union and health and safety duties and training.

This combination of changes fostered growth in the professional unions. Compared to the general unions, they had lower density rates and thus more capacity to recruit. Change and insecurity led professionals to seek protection; they were also growing in numbers. The legislative changes encouraged the professional unions to establish a network of stewards and health and safety representatives. Their activity led to increased sources of recruitment and more active branches. In the professional unions the industrial relations departments took on a more active role. Dyson and Spary (1979) refer to a move from professional interests by these organisations towards trade union interests. Professional interests have always reinforced trade union interest – the two are not separable. The move is best seen as one towards increased, and more devolved, use of the method of collective bargaining.

The Webbs (1917:36) give an insight into such unions when they discuss the 'Motives for Organisation'. Two of the motives are what they call the 'Creative Impulse' and the 'Possessive Impulse'. The creative is to do with the need to advance the art and science of their vocation; the possessive is to do with gaining as much remuneration and status as they can. The creative may be altruistic, but it can reinforce the possessive by increasing the body of knowledge required for entry, thus making the profession more exclusive. The working out of some of these forces is best illustrated by a case study.

*The Royal College of Midwives.* The professional unions have similar, but not identical, governance systems. The overwhelming impression is of highly centralised bodies geared at best to central pay determination and dealing with local individual cases on grievance an disciplinary matters, but deeply divided between the allocation of income for collective bargaining purposes such as more and better trained stewards and for professional and educational purposes. The RCM is used as an example to provide more general insights into some of these points.

The RCM has just about doubled its size, from 17 465 members in 1979 to 36 327 in 1992. The RCM now claim to have a density of over 85 per cent This suggests a slowing down of the rate of growth for the future and has focused attention on structure and organisation as subscription income has become 80 per cent of total income. One response to this has been to invite a scrutiny report, the contents of which remain confidential, but there are proposals for change emerging. The RCM has three main functional activities, all of which have to be administered and funded. These activities are designated as professional, educational and employment affairs. As indicated earlier, the college is registered as a trade union whilst the Royal College of Midwives Trust is registered as a charitable company. The general secretary is cast as secretary of a company and general secretary of a trade union. She is also known as the chief midwife. There is a notion that the trust covers education activities, the trade union covers industrial relations activities and that professional activities are overlapped by both.

Historically the council has been the supreme governing body of the college. Members are elected for three years with a requirement for national representation from the four countries of Northern Ireland, Scotland, Wales and England, beyond which there is no requirement for regional representation. There is an annual branch delegate conference attended by delegates from the 214 branches which does pass resolutions, but the council has not regarded itself as bound by these. At the 1993 conference there was a resolution that the council should be so bound. Suffice to say that there is healthy debate about where power lies and where it ought to lie with some drive for constitutional change.

Branch size ranges from around 20 members to over 600. Although branches are predominantly geographically based, branch activity is closely linked to workplaces. Stewards generally express concern about apathy but branch participation rates of around 8 per cent compare favourably with other unions. There is a tendency to see the branch as the forum for all workplace issues and not simply as a unit of government of the RCM. This leads to problems with members who are managers. As trusts develop there appears to be a tendency to identify the need to deal with workplace issues at meetings of those directly affected by work changes rather than simply through branch meetings.

The shift towards collective bargaining as a method has created problems for members of the RCM who are employed as managers and this is reflected throughout all the other professional unions. As senior professionals the managers see themselves as guardians of the creative impulse and challenges to their decisions – on, for example, such things as grade mix – are often seen as questioning superior professional judgements. The dilemma can become more acute when the challenge comes from senior line management with financial constraints as opposed to junior members with cost of living constraints. Codes of conduct and their supervision further complicate issues. Supervisors of midwives often have line management authority over those professionally supervised. They also have professional obligations under the code for midwives but may be managed by those without. The spectre of professional misconduct complicates disciplinary issues and grievance matters. In hearings managers find themselves challenged by officers of their own union and may feel betrayed by them to an extent that does not happen in other vertically organised unions.

That there may be a conflict between professional and industrial relations objectives has been reflected in the 1993 delegate conference. RCM annual reports state the aims of the college in terms which clearly underline the creative impulse: 'to advance the art and science of midwifery and to raise the efficiency and protect the interests of midwives'. However the conference passed the following resolution: 'In the NHS in the mid-1990s it is imperative that midwives are represented by a well resourced trade union dedicated to protecting their interests. It therefore calls upon Council to amend the College's aims and objectives to make this explicit.' At the place of work the potential conflict between these impulses can take quite subtle forms. The creative impulse leads to attempts to incorporate developments in practice. Team midwifery, which emphasises continuity of care by members of a team, has become a theme, its content based on reported experiments, particularly in the USA. What our research showed was that no two midwives involved in what was called team midwifery in different parts of the country had a coherent or consistent definition of its practice. The Institute of Manpower Studies (1993) suggests similar findings. At the place of work there is evidence of management using the demand for such practice as a way of achieving seven-day, three-shift working systems and degrading the skill mix. (In general nursing there is concern that patient-focused care is being used as a device for securing more flexible working.)

The three functions mentioned earlier in this section are 'allocated' to three departments: education, professional and employment affairs. These compete for influence and resources and given the powers of the council, the process which produces the outcomes is not always explicit. Revenues provided by the education department are in decline as a result of clinical education moving more generally into colleges of higher education and trusts identifying more economic ways of providing statutory refresher courses. In the decade to 1994, the balance of resources was shifting towards employment affairs.

It would appear from this latter point that it is the method of collective bargaining which has been attracting members. The number of industrial relations officers moved from three to 13 FTEs in the period under consideration. A northern office has been established and working from home introduced to allow for a more regional service to help meet the demands of devolved bargaining. To deal with the tendency of the impulses to come into conflict occasionally, consideration is being given to a closer relationship between the professional and employment affairs departments. (There has even been reference to the concept of a 'holistic' officer.) A factor which could have both an integrating and conciousness-raising effect is a recent move by the RCM to recognise a TUC-affiliated union to represent its own staff.

In 1995, the employment affairs department was restructured and placed under the leadership of the professional department. Newly recruited employment affairs staff were required to be qualified midwives. An arrangement was also reached with the MSF for the training of RCM stewards and access to MSF research. This effectively reduced the influence of the employment affairs department (see Burchill 1995). Between 1979 and 1992, the total number of representatives increased from 400 to 750, approximately 350 of these being separate health and safety representatives. Traditional theories of trade union growth are sufficient to explain current membership trends. Derecognition of the RCM at trust level is not something that managers would find sustainable. The growth of health care provision, whether private, public or both, now appears to be more problematic. Competition from other unions for membership hardly seems a problem for the RCM. Loss of jobs to health care assistants is likely to be offset by a widening of their role – probably at the expense of obstetricians and general practitioners – a point referred to earlier.

A factor influencing the rapid growth of RCM membership in the late 1980s appears to have been the clinical grading review. The two did coincide and the grading of midwives produced more discontent and a higher proportion of appeals amongst those groups affected by it. A factor affecting the supply of midwives appears to have been a consequence of issues emerging from the review. A midwifery qualification was claimed to be a second registrable qualification, over and above Registered General Nurse, and therefore two qualifications were needed to perform the task of midwife. In 1989, only a dozen or so midwives were trained on a direct entry basis each year. That figure is now 800 – out of a total of 2000. This makes it cheaper to train midwives but would appear to reduce their flexibility At the time of the clinical grading review, the RCM industrial relations department (now employment affairs) conducted a vigorous campaign within the profession to secure a separate pay structure for midwives. This proposal was opposed by the RCN. Both the RCM campaign and the RCN opposition are believed to have had an impact on membership. There are still funds set aside in the RCM accounts to examine the possibility of developing a job evaluation scheme specific to midwifery – a forlorn ambition in the light of devolved bargaining and trust emphases on continuous spine pay structures. Nevertheless it does illustrate the distinctive view the midwives have of their profession. There are other factors which might affect growth and retention of members which are still being researched. Evidence indicates a growing proportion of part-time midwives, greater incidence of redundancy and increased dependency on income from their employment as midwives.

This section has indicated some of the issues arising within professional unions. It has suggested that growth reflects, to some extent, those forces promoting collective bargaining. As indicated earlier, the method of mutual insurance cannot be ignored and, although high on reasons for joining, it is difficult to quantify relatively. Given that the employer is held liable, vicariously, for negligence it is hard to see why this is important. If individual liability became an issue, private practitioners would not secure indemnity within existing subscription rates. Probably more important is the provision of legal representation in UKCC hearings.

*Professional Unions: general issues.* The growth rate identified for the RCM is reflected in that of the other professional unions. They go completely against national trends and those of the general unions in the NHS. Some attempt has already been made to explain the trend for the professional unions. The more general unions started from a higher base of membership, and some of their traditional areas of recruitment have declined in employee numbers. As far as competition for membership between the professional unions is concerned, the RCN is the main predator. It actively seeks, and provides services for, midwives and health visitors. Beyond this, the professional unions tend to exclusivity. Membership of the RCM requires a midwifery qualification. The BMA is equally exclusive. UNISON, the MSF and the GMB have some professional membership. The main competition is between UNISON and the RCN. UNISON has a large nurse membership, but how many of these are professionally qualified is unknown. The introduction of HCAs into nursing and midwifery areas of work has led both the RCN and the RCM to consider recruiting them. Both, at this stage, have decided not to recruit HCAs. This could be taken to reflect the view that for the foreseeable future these unions see exclusivity and limited size as more instrumental to their purposes. All of the professional unions have made some response to the anticipated onset of more devolved bargaining.

The second largest professional union is the BMA (see Table 3.1). Like the RCN it has showed a continuous increase in membership over the period. The BMA suggest a density of approximately 80 per cent. There has been a rapid growth in female membership. This latter point reflects a growing proportion of female entrants to the profession, recruitment strategy and the disproportionate effects of junior doctors' hours on females in that group. BMA members have been very much at the centre of current reforms. The traditional issue of junior doctors' hours has continued to provide a major source of discontent. New contractual arrangements have been introduced for consultants. GP fundholding and the establishment of clinical directorates have further engaged BMA members. Not surprisingly, membership has increased over the period. The BMA employs a team of industrial relations officers (IROS) – highly qualified and experienced practitioners. Until the mid-1980s these were based on regions, one officer to each region, and the number had remained at 17 for a long period of time. There are now 24 IROs. The number of place of work accredited representatives (POWARs) is approximately 500. Because of the high degree of centralisation of pay bargaining the role of the POWARs was seen predominantly as

TABLE 3.1    *Membership of the professional unions*

| Union | 1980 | 1992 |
|-------|------|------|
| ACB | 1 862 | 2 372 |
| BMA | 65 650 | 88 107 |
| RCM | 18 762 | 36 327 |
| HVA | 13 496 | 15 118* |
| CSP | 20 191 | 25 408 |
| SoC | 4 547 | 5 879 |
| BDA (dental) | 13 132 | 15 106 |
| BDA (dietetic) | 2 220 | 3 061 |
| SoR | 9 119 | 12 931 |
| BAOT | 6 259 | 12 026 |
| HCSA | 4 300 | 2 400 |
| BOS | 665 | 1 342 |
| DNA | 1 500 | 4 600 |
| RCN | 16 1962 | 293 193 |
| HPA | 902 | 1 524 |

*Note:*   *merged with MSF 1989.
*Source:*   Certification Office, except DNA, Head Office.

representing individuals in grievance and disciplinary matters. In practice IROs performed these functions.

With the drive towards more decentralised bargaining the BMA has altered its local structure. Local negotiating committees of four or five members, plus an IRO, are being established and this will greatly increase the number of active representatives. Traditionally the BMA has not participated in local joint consultative committees, although currently the view is that such participation can be regarded as a fall-back position. To facilitate this the BMA has intensified its training programme. All of this suggests a more active role for the BMA in local bargaining affairs.

Similar trends can be identified in the other organisations, apart from the HCSA, which has lost members to the BMA. In the last decade the BAOT has increased its IROs from 2 to 11; its stewards from 200 to 566 and, since 1987 its Health and Safety representatives from 100 to 348. These trends in numbers of officers are apparent in all organisations except the HCSA. In its evidence to the employment committee, the RCN states that it 'has 480 staff located both in the RCN Headquarters and in the 20 local offices throughout the UK. It has 76 officers with labour relations responsibilities working alongside 3,000 RCN Stewards and 2,000 Safety Representatives. The RCN has over 261 branches throughout the UK'. It attributes its growth to 'the choice of individual nurses for the services which we offer.' They also take the view that provision of these services is independent of recognition and that loss of recognition would not lead to loss of membership.

Factors affecting union growth in general have already been referred to. The period under consideration appears to show increases associated with pay review body membership. This could be boosted by the 1994 government response to this body. In their evidence to the employment committee, the RCN quote the *Financial Times*:

> The RCN has doubled in size by offering an impressive range of professional services. It runs a political lobbying operation with a record in stirring up public support for nurses which chills the marrow of NHS employers and ministers. And nurses have shot up the pay league since the RCN won its appeal for clinical grading, without a single day lost through strikes.

Whatever the relationship, and whatever the causes, the RCN currently has a dynamic which the TUC affiliates do not have. A reasonable guess would be that they will continue to increase as a result of more nurses joining in general and at the expense of the TUC affiliates. This, for the foreseeable future, should offset the decline in the number of qualified nurses in employment. The latter will affect the dynamic referred to above and the increased presence of the RCN at the place of work. This is a direct consequence of growth but there are also indirect consequences. The number of full-time officers and the number of workplace representatives have increased along with the training and research back-up. These changes work towards reinforcing the growth trend.

Apart from increasing its collective bargaining support services, the RCN has approved changes in its branch structure. While it has retained its geographical branches, 'associated branches' have been established in what are called local employment units (LEUs). LEUs consist of trusts and the remaining directly managed units. This is something similar to the chapel/branch structure associated with unions in what was the print industry. Branches have conveners and LEUs have lead stewards. Suffice it to say that the trends in membership, officers, officer training and research in these organisations, combined with an increased interest in involvement at the place of work, will lead to these organisations playing a greater role. These factors, combined with the skills associated with the professions and the fact that UNISON will be looking inwards for a period, suggest that some of this will be at the expense of the more general unions.

The pressures on union structure stemming from devolved bargaining have made some of the smaller professional unions examine their position. Not much has happened in practice although there are several important developments in midstream. The Society of Remedial Gymnasts joined the CSP in 1985 – a transfer of 800 members. In 1993, the Hospital Physicists Association voted to merge with the MSF, transferring approximately 1600 members. More important was the merger of the HVA with the MSF in 1990. This not only involved a larger transfer, 15 000 members, it was of considerable strategic importance in that it brought the MSF into the organisation of staff associated with nursing. The BAOT has transferred the provision of its industrial relations services to UNISON. Prior to this it had been involved with the physiotherapists, the radiographers, the dieticians, the orthoptists and the chiropodists in negotiations to establish a separate union which would deal with the industrial relations requirements of these organisations while leaving the professional and college activities separate but intact. Such a strategy does not fit the analysis of the Webbs which suggests that these functions are inextricably intertwined. In a similar way the biochemists have sought to secure external provision of industrial relations services from larger general unions. The DNA, with an eye to the future, has changed its name to the Community and District Nursing Association and is working with GMB/APEX as a bargaining partner.

The SoR and the CSP have affiliated to the TUC. This also represents a response to the pressures of change in the NHS. Both organisations have seen this move as a way of gaining access to TUC services which can, for example, provide regionally based training of stewards. A difficulty here is that such training becomes less specialised. In some cases joint training of full-time officers and stewards of TUC and non-TUC organisations has taken place, illustrating the growing links. These developments do represent the problems faced by the smaller organisations as bargaining devolves. National officers and central offices could cope with Whitley pure and simple, but not necessarily with more devolved bargaining. The HVA merger with MSF reflected circumstances which were quite special and although the choice of MSF has been rationalised in terms of MSF's local bargaining expertise it also had a lot to do with internal management difficulties related to inadequate computerisation of subscriptions.

A factor which could soon complicate the whole picture is the rapid development of the use of recently developed medical technology. This allows for less traumatic forms of surgery. Day case interventions are increasing rapidly as a proportion of all interventions. Their increase results in the need for fewer, possibly larger, hospitals, reducing the need to provide 'hotel facilities' and increasing the intensity of the care of inpatients. It has been predicted that by the year 2000 the number of hospital beds in the UK will reduce by half. This, along with newer technology, has profound implications for the distribution of health care and for the future membership and organisation of both the professional and the general unions. (See Newchurch, Health Briefing 1993.)

**Conclusion**

We can safely assume that Whitleyism, as associated with the NHS, has completely broken down, the settlements of 1995 being the final blow. It is hard to conceive of any meaningful future role for the PRBs.

The professional unions could well have reached a plateau in terms of membership growth. Trust closures, and mergers on a large scale, will cause a considerable fall in the number of NHS staff, and this will affect all unions. New technology, and the emphasis on the community as the base for provision, will affect the structure of the labour force in terms of training and skills, and their actual location in geographical terms. Unions in the health service will face problems similar to those faced by unions elsewhere. Local bargaining is coinciding with a considerable weakening of union bargaining power as a consequence of the reforms referred to.

In the short run the general and professional unions are

working together. At trust level they have collaborated on the development of new bargaining arrangements. As indicated above, they have arranged some joint training programmes. The RCN, RCM and CSP are all examining their policies on industrial action.

# 4

# Industrial Relations at the Place of Work

It was suggested in Chapter 3 that two main features of Whitley-ism were highly centralised bargaining supplemented by joint consultation at the place of work. A consequence of the adoption of the Whitley system in the NHS is that the existence of consultative machinery at the place of work is virtually universal. In practice this means that there is provision for regular meetings between management and recognised unions at what are generally referred to as 'joint consultative committees' (JCCs). Inevitably the structure of such committees, the content of their activity, the degree of participation of recognised unions and the regularity of meetings will vary. Nevertheless there are basic principles which seem to apply quite generally. Meetings tend to be arranged quarterly. Staff-side unions arrange pre-meetings to establish common policies in respect of agenda items. Participants regard the committees as performing functions which are of importance.

The theory underlying joint consultation tends to emphasise the notion of improving decision making by the passing of information. In its purest form management informs the workforce representatives of any changes they intend to introduce outside of basic terms and conditions of employment and adjust their proposals in the light of responses from these representatives. In the process, management reserve their right to make the final decision. The section of the NHS Whitley Agreement which deals with joint consultation incorporates a quotation from McCarthy (1976): 'It should be accepted that the mere passage of information is not consultation. Consultation involves an opportunity to influence decisions and their application. It is best conducted when some attention has been given to alternatives, but they have not taken their final form.'

Obviously it is difficult to identify in practice any change which does not impinge on pay and terms and conditions in some way or another. For example, the introduction of car parking charges for staff is an item which in recent years has regularly appeared on JCC agenda throughout the NHS. Such items inevitably produce negotiated settlements. One consequence of the overlap between negotiation and consultation is that a number of NHS units refer to joint negotiating and consultative committees.

The main purpose of this chapter is to identify what goes on at the place of work in terms of dealing with those issues which divide management and staff in the areas of pay, terms and conditions of employment, and anything else for that matter. Management are keen to control costs and increase productivity. The labour force is keen to improve pay and working conditions. These issues are now predominantly being determined at the place of work rather than through central negotiations. In general theoretical terms we are looking at the rules which govern the workplace and how these are determined. The law has a lot to say about rules relating to health and safety. Some unions, as indicated in Chapter 3, are regulated in their behaviour by statutory codes of conduct which inhibit management control. A way towards disentangling the processes involved is to take our trust as a case study and to try to separate what is determined at the place of work and the machinery used for such determination. It will also allow us to examine the main changes taking place in the NHS and how these changes are being responded to in terms of the rule-making process.

### Staff Consultative Arrangements

There is in place a hospital staff consultative committee (HSCC). It is worth examining and commenting on its main provisions. It begins with a 'Mission Statement':

> Maximising effective use of all facilities in order to provide a comprehensive range of acute services for local residents and create opportunities to serve a wider population.

* Quality matters to our customers and to us.
* Our staff are our most important resource.
* We aim to be best in all that we do.

The above is the mission statement of the hospital and is included as a reminder in the constitution of the HSCC. Storey and Sisson (1993:179–84) discuss the origins and intent of such statements. Obvious intentions can be to create a sense of purpose and team spirit. The above statement mentions customers rather than patients and could be seen to be inculcating a sense of market forces. Anybody with any relationship with the NHS would realise that notions of acquiring commitment and so on, also associated with such statements, may not be as relevant as in other industries. NHS staff have a tradition of putting patients first, often at their own expense. Where the introduction of such statements coincides with job losses, closures and increases in work intensity it can have effects opposite to those intended.

In our trust, the opening of a new hospital, and all that goes with such an enterprise, generated a sense of achievement and community. Mission statements are no substitute for actual achievement. Whether they aid achievement or otherwise is not supported by any clear evidence.

*Aims*

The aims of the HSCC are expressed as follows:

1 To be an important consultation and communication forum complementary to the Directorate and Departmental Management System.
2 To provide employees with opportunity to influence and be involved in decisions which are likely to affect their interests and the working of the Unit.
3 To help the Unit meet the needs of its clients using the skills and knowledge of its staff.

This is a classic statement of the aims of joint consultation. It fits the definition incorporated in the General Whitley Council provisions. The approach is further reinforced by the following:

Functions

1   To provide a forum for consultation between staff interests and senior management.
2   To share information on matters affecting the NHS, the Health Authority and the Unit.
3   To promote co-operation between staff and managers on matters of general staff interest.
4   To co-operate on matters of local Terms and Conditions and local policies affecting staff.
5   The Agendae [*sic*] will cover operational change and key strategic issues, eg. Business Planning, Commissioning of District General Hospital, Culture of Unit, Communication Systems, Planning of Services, Quality of Service, new practices and developments affecting staff.

A feature of the concept of 'joint' consultation is that it is meant generally, and certainly in the NHS, to incorporate the notion of representative bodies being involved. In other words, consulting with individuals, even if all individuals are consulted with, does not fulfil the requirement for joint consultation. This is reflected in the section dealing with membership of the HSCC.

Membership

1   The HSCC shall consist of up to 18 members, 12 of whom will be elected by the staff side, and 6 representing the Management Side. The total number may be varied by mutual agreement.
2   Staff Side members will be Accredited Union Representatives of Trade Unions and Professional Organisations.
3   The Management Side will consist of 6 representatives including the Chief Executive.

The membership indicates a number of things: trade unions are recognised; there is a shop steward structure; management is represented at the most senior line level. There is also a provision in the constitution for the staff side to hold monthly meetings of their own to prepare for the meetings of the HSCC. The HSCC meetings take place on a quarterly basis. Staff side representatives are provided with office, filing, photocopying and telephone facilities.

Unions recognised include UNISON, RCN, RCM, BAOT, MSF, British Dietetic Association, CSP, SoR, AEEU and BMA. These are all recognised at GWC level, and are the GWC unions which exist at our trust site. Of these, the BMA does not participate in the HSCC. This reflects BMA policy of remaining aloof from such committees and seeking to deal separately with issues as they affect them. At national level the policy of the BMA, reflecting NHS changes, is to try to establish, at unit levels, local negotiating committees of four or five members, plus one of their industrial relations officers.

*Agenda*

An examination of agenda items and minutes of the HSCC shows a wide range of issues listed and openly discussed. Invariably the first item was the financial position of the trust. Sub-committees, made up of equal management and staff-side membership, reported back on such matters as equal opportunities policies, recognition, disciplinary and grievance procedures, statutory holiday entitlements and so on. Matters such as lists of vacancies and frozen posts were tabled and discussed. The introduction of an attendance policy raised serious discussion which produced agreement. This policy was mainly concerned with short term absences and trying to set a target of a 4 per cent maximum. Controlling absenteeism is linked to human resource planning, as discussed in Chapter 1. The rate of absenteeism influences required staffing levels. Recent legislative change has removed government contributions to sick pay, thus making sickness absence more costly for the employer. This concern with attendance levels is widely reflected throughout the NHS.

Other items which recurred related to such things as training and the introduction of health care assistants (HCAs). The latter issue was linked to a work reprofiling exercise conducted with nurses and midwives. Although these form a distinct group, and constitute a directorate, progress on this exercise was regularly reported back to the HSCC. Communications within this group were facilitated by a nurses and midwives forum. Such a forum represents the kind of directorate and departmental communications mechanism referred to above under the first aim of the HSCC constitution.

The trust has a health and safety committee (see Chapter 5). Items of broad general importance under this heading were brought to the HSCC. These included such things as security, smoking and alcohol policies and EU regulations on manual handling and VDUs. Policies such as HIV/AIDS and employment were also discussed – these overlap health and safety and equal opportunities. Basically the health and safety committee is expected to report back to the HSCC.

## Consultation and Negotiation

There is a fine dividing line in practice between these two concepts. Consultation suggests a set of management objectives which are only modified in the light of information which improves the content of these objectives or their achievability. Ultimately it is management who decide. Within a unitarist philosophy everybody would benefit, even though the process involves no compromise by management. Negotiation implies compromise between parties who have conflicting objectives. For example, if the objective of a union is to secure a pay increase of 5 per cent and the employer wishes to achieve 4 per cent, it is not possible for both sides to achieve their objectives. One or other or both must compromise.

Walton and McKersie (1965) distinguish between *integrative* and *distributive* bargaining. Integrative bargaining situations tend to be associated with the possibility of both sides gaining from problem solving. The reorganisation of a shift pattern might result in both parties benefiting, although it has to be recognised that there might be a conflict over the share of benefits. In distributive bargaining, one side benefits at the expense of the other.

The consultation process might not be expressed in terms of compromise, but the final outcome may result in compromise. Views expressed by the workforce might be seen by management to reflect a strength of feeling which they wish to avoid being registered. If they respond in a way which varies from their initial objectives, have they compromised or simply taken on board information? How do we clearly distinguish between negotiating bodies and consultative bodies? Seifert (1992:8) says: 'Consultation tends to be what it says it is, namely seeking out the opinion of others to suggestions without any obligation to take any notice.' This raises the obvious question. Are there any situations in which one is obliged to take notice of the opinions of others?

Opinions are taken notice of because they help to secure objectives, or because, if ignored, they might generate retaliation and opposition. There is also the question of what exactly 'taking notice of opinions' really means.

Examining the agenda of HSCCs in the NHS suggests that they deal with local issues, whatever those issues might be, which are not determined by Whitley or the pay review bodies at national level. The tone of minutes suggests a collaborative relationship, less overtly conflictual than that associated with bodies explicitly devoted to collective bargaining. For example, in negotiations at plant level, in other industries, an annual claim will often cover the range of issues incorporated in a traditional NHS HSCC with the addition of pay and hours. The formal inclusion of pay and hours gives a greater edge to such meetings.

HSCCs do incorporate negotiation and, as said at the beginning, sometimes explicitly in their title. They also pass financial information. Such information would be passed in negotiations – it is not specific to the consultation process. Negotiations almost invariably begin with what is usually described as a 'state of the nation' speech from the employer. The distinction is not between consultation and negotiation in NHS HSCCs; it is between what is determined nationally and what is determined locally, with HSCCs determining local issues. However HSCCs do not determine all local issues. The non-participation of the BMA has already been referred to. Similarly, at our trust there was a nurses and midwives forum. What are described as 'functional issues' – that is of specific concern to one group – are usually dealt with directly with such groups. Consultants' job plans are a matter for consultants; productivity agreements with portering and catering staff are negotiated directly with them, although the level of bonus might have been nationally determined in the past. Clearly local pay determination is set to change the role of HSCCs.

## Decentralised Bargaining

The prospect of local pay determination, and eventually its actuality, have already produced a plethora of responses at trust level. Examining these and potential variations gives insight into the process of industrial relations at the place of work. Given the

HSCC arrangements outlined above, an approach would be simply to extend the agenda of such committees.

*Recognition*

The decentralisation of bargaining to Trust level replaces centralised multi-employer/multi-union bargaining with single employer/multi-union bargaining. Trusts, the single employers, are having to consider how to handle the large number of unions which exists in the NHS and in most trusts. Several options are being explored. There is very little evidence of serious attempts at derecognition. Unions such as the BMA and RCN are so powerful that derecognition of trade unions as a matter of principle is currently not feasible. Most trusts are seeking ways of rationalising negotiating procedures which allow them to deal more effectively with their multi-union situations. One approach is to replicate Whitley at local level. The HSCC deals with issues of common concern and oversees all developments, with groups of workers dealt with on issues specific to them by functional arrangements. Ambulance staff, nursing staff, midwifery staff, medical staff, ancillary staff and so on would be dealt with separately, through their recognised unions, but would meet at HSCC level on common issues. (For examples of these, see Chapter 10.)

This is basically the approach adopted by our trust and outlined above. The question to be answered is whether this machinery can cope with pay and terms and conditions as an add on. Pragmatically most trusts will be starting from this position and perhaps seeking ways forward. The route they take is likely to be decided pragmatically: according to tradition, the strengths of the trade unions, the aspirations and abilities of managers and the force of competition and downward pressures from the NHS hierarchy. NHS strategy documents have proposed variations for consideration. It has been suggested that trusts might try for single union recognition. Given the diversity of occupation and the strength of individual unions this is unlikely to be practicable for most trusts. A suggestion that the number of unions recognised be reduced by identifying 'prime' unions also has problems. This would involve recognising larger unions and expecting them to negotiate on behalf of others. Examples would perhaps be to recognise the RCN as bargaining on behalf of nurses, midwives and health visitors. Such a tactic would exclude the RCM and HVA. UNISON might be recognised as dealing with all other staff to the exclusion of MSF, GMB and TGWU. In both cases there would be problems. The strength of professional unions can be very great even though they are small. Grievance and disciplinary issues can require highly specialised representation.

Another potential development is partial recognition. The question of recognition and the degree of recognition overlaps with the question of bargaining structures. Before examining bargaining structures it is worth making a point about an aspect of recognition in the NHS. There has been a tradition of the employer collecting contributions from union members, on behalf of recognised unions, through the system of deduction of contributions at source (DOCAS), sometimes referred to as the check-off arrangement. Under this system union contributions are deducted from wages with the permission of the member.

The Trade Union Reform and Employment Rights Act 1993 (TURERA) required that from August 1993 each member must renew consent for such deductions at least every three years. This created a tremendous administrative burden on unions who needed then to pursue members to renew consent. It also gave employers the occasion to review such procedures and recognition itself. Our trust has decided to co-operate with those unions affected rather than review arrangements, although it took the opportunity to impose an administrative charge for the DOCAS service. Not all unions are affected evenly. Many professional unions operated on a direct debit basis to collect subscriptions.

*Bargaining Structures*

The arrangements for bargaining over pay and terms and conditions on an annual basis could be partially separated from the HSCC structure. Bargaining separately with each union over annual agreements can be bureaucratic and time consuming. It can also lead to unions delaying outcomes in anticipation of other union deals and to leapfrogging claims on the basis of such outcomes.

The existing HSCC could be used as the basis for recognition. Sub-committees have already been referred to as a device for agreeing procedures on such things as discipline, grievance and grading procedures. A device proposed in a number of trusts is that the HSCC unions themselves agree a team of negotiators – perhaps four – from the whole membership of the HSCC. This negotiating team would meet management to deal with basic terms and conditions. From this arrangement, agreements would be reached on a 'single table bargaining' basis. Single table bargaining involves all unions simultaneously – in our case represented by four nominees – negotiating with management, with recommendations being put jointly to all the members represented, regardless of union. There would be only one vote on behalf of all members, rather than separate union votes. How such a procedure would work remains to be seen. Such an approach has been seen as facilitating the harmonisation of terms and conditions and the establishment of single status arrangements. It has also been seen as helpful in achieving flexibility – see Marginson and Sisson (1990).

It will be interesting to see whether or not such bargaining settles down at trust level, or somewhere higher. Competition for labour between trusts could at some future date result in trusts collaborating at local level to establish common terms and prevent leapfrogging pay claims. The process of trust mergers is moving at such a rapid pace that units for bargaining purposes are becoming quite large as well as geographically distanced – our trust is being taken over by a trust with a hospital located ten miles away from our trust's new hospital.

*Procedures*

The possibility of moving away from Whitley has already led to fairly widespread renegotiating of procedures relating to discipline and grievances. Others, like the HSCC procedure and health and safety have so far remained relatively intact. In between are procedures which determine pay structures, such as job evaluation, where national schemes are still in place but with some growth in local variation. This section will examine the nature of these procedures and the changes at play.

*Disciplinary Procedures.* Local disciplinary procedures have been in the process of renegotiation over a number of years, in many cases since the early 1970s. The pattern which is emerging in the

NHS is very similar to that in industry in general. This reflects the impact of unfair dismissal legislation. A complicating factor in the NHS is the existence of codes of conduct and supervisory bodies for professional staff. Professional misconduct and competence will be of interest to bodies such as the UKCC and the GMC.

Given that professional misconduct or incompetence can lead to a situation where a person not only loses a job, but may never be able to practise again, it is not surprising that disciplinary action can be regarded more seriously in NHS contexts than perhaps elsewhere. It also means that the individual may be dealt with by two procedures – the internal trust procedure and the external professional procedure. This section is mainly concerned with the internal procedure, but it is worth noting at least one complication to give an insight into some of the issues. The professional conduct of midwives is overseen by a supervisor of midwives, appointed in accordance with the midwives rules, issued by the UKCC. It often happens that such supervisors are managers with line authority over those they supervise. In such a situation the midwife might find that the first stage of internal disciplinary action is under the control of somebody with external authority through the UKCC requirements. A supervisor of midwives is not a supervisor in the traditional management sense. As such the supervisor has no line authority at the place of work, although it is possible that in her work role she may well have.

Separating the professional issues from employment issues is difficult; employees of all types in the NHS are governed by rules relating to conduct, performance and capability. Here we will examine the main ingredients of the disciplinary procedure in our trust. For a general introduction to disciplinary procedures, see Burchill (1992:ch. 7). There is a legal background to discipline and associated procedures. The Employment Protection (Consolidation) Act 1978, as amended by TURERA 1993, requires the employer to provide written details of disciplinary procedures. Under the Employment Protection Act 1975, ACAS issued *Code of Practice No.1: Disciplinary practice and procedures in employment.* Failure to act in accordance with this code is taken into account by industrial tribunals. This code, combined with industrial tribunal decisions, has been very influential in determining the extent, nature and use of disciplinary procedures. It has been very influential in establishing standardisation in such matters.

A disciplinary procedure itself is very much a statement of sanctions available which can be imposed in relation to matters of misconduct, poor performance and incapability. Such procedures are usually supported by an agreed code for the handling of disciplinary issues. The code is designed to achieve agreed standards of 'fairness' in the application of standards. As already mentioned, the procedure and code at our trust was agreed at the HSCC, having been developed by a sub-committee of it. The procedure tells us:

> In many situations counselling may be a more satisfactory method of resolving problems than disciplinary action.
>
> The purpose of counselling will be to establish whether there are any problems facing the employee with which he or she can be helped and to ensure that the employee is aware of the standards required. The emphasis should be on finding ways to help the employee improve.

Counselling is on a one-to-one basis between the first line manager and the employee. It is expected to give clear guidance, be recorded and, if the employee wishes, a written note should be given to him or her. Since it does not constitute disciplinary action there is no right to be represented. Where disciplinary action is undertaken, at whatever level of sanction, the employee has the right to be represented by a trade union representative or a work colleague. No disciplinary action can be taken against a trade union representative without prior discussion with a full-time trade union officer.

The lowest level of sanction is an oral warning, and this is described as stage 1. Stage 2 consists of a first written warning; stage 3, a final written warning; stage 4, dismissal. Stages 1 and 2 contain the following requirements: 'The employee's manager will take steps to establish and gather all the relevant facts and will hold an investigatory/disciplinary hearing. He/she will take advice from the Unit Personnel Officer prior to any hearing.' For stages 3 and 4 it is required that advice be taken from the personnel director. The division between an investigatory and disciplinary hearing reflects two possible sets of circumstances. Where the employee, for example, admits to a charge, the hearing will consist of a plea in mitigation, which takes account of all surrounding circumstances, before action is decided. If the employee denies a charge, then a hearing will need to take place allowing all evidence to be examined by the parties. Where the decision is one of 'guilty', this investigatory hearing will usually be immediately followed by the disciplinary hearing – the plea in mitigation.

Depending upon how serious the issue is, the procedure might be entered at any stage. Performance and capability issues would generally be expected to follow the whole procedure through its various stages. Where written warnings are involved – Stages 2 and 3 – downgrading, relocation or change of duties may be given in addition. There is a right of appeal against any disciplinary sanction applied. Such appeals are heard by a committee of the trust board, consisting of three members, none of whom are associated with the area of management related to the issue. At least one member should be a non-executive.

In cases which involve gross misconduct, suspension with pay may be applied, pending the outcome of a disciplinary hearing. Gross misconduct usually warrants dismissal without notice – summary dismissal. The procedure refers to gross misconduct in the following terms: 'Gross misconduct includes such offences as theft, assault, fraud, deliberate damage to Trust property. There may be other instances of a similar gravity which would constitute gross misconduct.' Warnings carry time limits which allow them to expire. This means that no reference should be made to them in future disciplinary proceedings – no account should be taken of them. The time limit for an oral warning is 'up to 6 months'; for a first written warning, 'up to 12 months'; and for a final written warning, 'up to 2 years'.

Where a dismissal takes place, the individual has a right to take the matter to an industrial tribunal, where it can be claimed to be unfair. As suggested earlier, tribunals have had a considerable effect on both disciplinary procedures and practice. This is reflected above in the stages, the rights of employees to be heard and represented, the need for proper investigation and so on. There is not space here to examine all the elements of 'fairness'. The ACAS handbook, *Discipline at Work*, provides an excellent overall guide.

As far as conduct is concerned, the Employment Appeals Tribunal has laid down guidelines for employers in two important cases: *British Home Stores* v. *Burchell* (1978) and *Weddel & Co.* v. *Tepper* (1980). For an employee to be guilty of misconduct 'on the balance of probabilities' the employer must have (1) a genuine belief, (2) on reasonable grounds, (3) after reasonable investigation. It would, of course, be possible for a union to register a failure to agree with the dismissal of a member. The possibilities that this could give rise to will be discussed below. A consequence of devolving discipline to trust level is that appeals to district, region and in some cases the secretary of state are no longer provided for. The trust may be the final arbiter before an industrial tribunal is involved.

*Grievance Procedures.* The right to raise grievances at work and to knowledge of the grievance procedure is given the same statutory backing as that given to discipline. Each employee has the right to raise grievances at work and to know the procedure for doing so. A key issue to resolve is what exactly constitutes a grievance. Torrington and Hall (1991;p540) refer to a work by Pigors and Myers in 1977: ' "Grievance: A complaint that has been formally presented to a management representative or to a union official." This provides us with a useful categorization by separating out *grievance* as a formal, relatively drastic step, compared with commonplace grumbling.' The implication of Torrington and Hall's analysis is that anything which is formally raised is a grievance. This evades certain issues in connection with what is essentially a technical term. A useful definition of a grievance is the one incorporated in the International Labour Organisation (ILO) Recommendation, number 130, adopted in 1967:

> the grounds for a grievance may be any measure or situation which concerns the relations between employer and worker or which affects or may affect the conditions of employment of one or several workers in the undertaking when that measure or situation appears contrary to provisions of an applicable collective agreement or of an individual collective agreement or of an individual contract of employment, to works rules, to laws or regulations or to the custom or usage of the occupation, branch of economic activity or country, regard being had to principles of good faith.

What this definition suggests is that grievances are about breaches of rights – rights determined by agreements, laws and rules. A grievance should incorporate a claim that rights are being breached under one or other of these headings. Obviously there are difficulties. If all such rights were clearly expressed, grievances would be easily settled. Custom and practice are not always clear; neither is good faith. Disputes over grievances usually derive from failures to agree over interpretation. Even legal duties on employers contain some notion of 'reasonableness' – a term open to interpretation.

The definition does, however, clearly indicate that debates about whether or not a genuine grievance exists will revolve around the concept of 'rights' and will refer to rules and natural justice. Grievance procedures rarely allow 'grumbles' or 'complaints' to be progressed. The literature does distinguish between 'disputes of right' and 'disputes of interest'. Disputes of right (grievances) are about what the rules mean; disputes of interest are about what the rules should be. Disputes of interest are usually failures to agree about what a new agreement should contain.

Our trust grievance procedure begins with a definition of a grievance clearly derived from the ILO recommendation:

> For the purposes of the procedure 'grievance' means: 'a claim by employee(s) or a trade union concerning the employee(s)' individual or collective rights under the applicable collective agreement, individual contract of employment, law, regulation, works rules, custom or practice...' Such claims involve questions relating to the interpretation or application of the rules concerned.

It is worth noting that a grievance is always 'against' management or the employer. If a fellow employee is the source of a grievance – sexual harassment, for example – it is management's duty to protect employees from such behaviour.

One of the consequences of decentralisation and NHS reform is that there has been a drastic change in NHS grievance procedures. The term is used in the plural because Whitley had provided a procedure for individual issues, the grievance procedure, and a procedure for collective grievances, the disputes procedure. Notionally the disputes procedure dealt with grievances involving more than one person. This distinction is a commonplace one in industry generally, but in practice difficult to sustain. If grievances revolve around the interpretation of rules, the outcome for an individual will set a precedent for others. What is emerging in the NHS at trust level is a single procedure for dealing with all grievances; this is also the case in our trust. Both the Whitley procedures consisted of numerous stages up to national level. These could be longwinded and frustrating. In 1988, when clinical grading was introduced, appeals against proposed gradings were put into the then existing grievance procedure. Six years later, 5000 appeals were still in procedure to establish gradings for 1 April 1988.

Trusts are generally introducing grievance procedures with three formal internal stages. Before entering the procedure an employee who believed that s/he had a grievance would try to settle the matter with the first line manager. If this was not possible the first formal stage of the procedure would be to return to the line manager with representation, if required. Representation would be by a union representative or colleague. Stage 2 would be to the departmental or functional manager, and stage 3 to the trust general manager. In our trust each of these stages is expected to take no more than five days. The final stage is to a committee of the trust board, with a time limit of three weeks.

It is always possible to fail to agree at the final stage of either the disciplinary or the grievance procedure. Notionally this could result in industrial action. The possibility of taking industrial action is considerably constrained by the law in the UK. Even where the requirements of the law are fulfilled, individuals may not be protected. Employees may be summarily dismissed for taking strike action, for example, regardless of whether or not the strike is lawful. There are some minimum constraints on employers in such circumstances.

This is not a text which allows for a discussion in detail of the law relating to industrial action – this is best pursued by the reader elsewhere. Whatever the constraints, industrial action does take place. Procedures and practices are generally designed to support and develop co-operative and productive work practices. Failures to agree may require additional approaches. A few trusts have extended their procedures to involve third parties where such failures occur. Where this has been done, the extension usually applies to all failures including those arising out of pay negotiations – disputes of interest, as well as disputes of right. In our trust, the use of a third party is confined to grading appeals, which would be classified as disputes of right (see below).

There are three main options for dealing with failures to agree, over and above simply facing the consequences. These can be incorporated in procedures, or used on an ad hoc basis. Before examining the options we need to look at the possible 'trigger mechanisms', the form of words used to allow for the invocation of third party involvement. The terminology below is useful in making important distinctions:

**Compulsory**　'If the parties fail to agree the matter *will* be referred to...'

**Unilateral**　'If the parties fail to agree, *either* party may refer the matter to...' In this case if one party wishes to go to a third party the other must also participate.

**Voluntary**　'If the parties fail to agree, the matter *may* be referred to... if both parties agree to do so.' In this formulation, if one party refuses to go to a third party, then the matter must be resolved in some other way. This last formulation simply acts as a reminder to the parties that there is somewhere else to go.

The unilateral approach is fairly widely used in respect of *conciliation*. In the context of a failure to agree, this form of conciliation is described as 'collective' to distinguish it from 'individual' conciliation which is usually associated with attempts to settle industrial tribunal cases without going to a full hearing. Conciliators have no powers to make either formal recommendations or decisions. Their role is to bring the parties together, perhaps suggest options the parties had not thought of, or even to provide a fresh negotiating arena. It can be entered into with or without commitment: one party may have no intention of moving from its previously established position.

Conciliation can be an extremely useful device. It might bring new information; it allows propositions to be tested through a third party, thus diluting the degree of commitment; it allows for negotiations to be reopened without loss of face. ACAS is most widely used for this, and for the other forms of intervention. For this particular form, ACAS uses its own full-time staff. In 1993,

ACAS completed collective conciliation action in 1118 cases. (ACAS *Annual Report 1993*). For other forms of intervention ACAS keeps a list of independent experts who are used on an ad hoc basis. The parties jointly agree persons whose names are submitted by ACAS. *Mediation* is a form of intervention in which the third party is asked to make recommendations. The parties, however, have not agreed to be bound by the recommendations. The terms of reference are often quite wide ranging and could refer to the whole of an annual pay, terms and conditions agreement. Mediation can provide a forum for both conciliation and negotiation. A mediator will usually seek out areas of agreement in respect of recommendations the parties will accept, and then try to identify forms of words which will settle the outstanding issues. Often the parties are seeking support for positions they wish to 'sell' to those they represent. In 1993, ACAS completed seven mediation cases. This is a low incidence, which is surprising given that it can be very helpful if used on an ad hoc basis. The NHS pay review bodies play the role of mediator, but without the continuation of the negotiating process. They invite evidence from the unions and the 'employers' and make recommendations to the parties and the ultimate NHS employer, the government. Neither the government nor the unions is bound by the recommendations. There is some evidence that the government is sensitive to the political problems it would face if seen to go too far below such recommendations, which are always made public.

*Arbitration* is based on an understanding by the parties that they will be bound by the decision of the arbitrator. Arbitration is most frequently triggered on an ad hoc basis. 'No strike deals' are those where a failure to agree automatically results in arbitration. Such deals are few and far between. The problem with such deals is that they tend to 'freeze' negotiations. No arbitrator would decide below a final offer or above a final demand. Although the practice of arbitrators is to settle very close to one or other of the final positions, and not 'split the difference', as is often presumed, it can still offer the temptation of a little more for the union. This knowledge can lead to the employer maintaining a position well below what they would be willing to concede and the union holding out for much more than they would ever hope to get.

What has become known in the UK as 'pendulum arbitration'

is a system of arbitration which requires the arbitrator to choose one or other of the final positions of the two parties. For example, if the issue were a straight pay claim with an employer final offer of 4 per cent and a union final demand of 7 per cent, the arbitrator must choose either 4 per cent or 7 per cent as the decision. It is believed that such a method closes the gap between them, because each party will be trying to establish a position which the arbitrator would perceive as reasonable. Notionally, the gap should become so narrow that a settlement occurs without arbitration. In 1993, ACAS reported 152 cases of arbitration. Of these, four were dealt with on a pendulum basis. Close to 80 per cent of all cases dealt with rights issues – dismissal, discipline and grading issues predominating – and 13 per cent of the cases dealt with annual pay.

There is a case for arbitration on rights issues where the arbitrator is giving an interpretation of existing agreements and practice. Where pay is concerned, ad hoc recourse to arbitration can be an effective way of resolving a difference after extended negotiations, as opposed to entering into mutually destructive action. It could be argued that the costs of no strike deals are worth bearing in an industry such as the NHS where action could have extreme consequences. On the other hand, most employees – in particular nursing and midwifery staff – who belong to professional unions did have union rules which prohibited industrial action. This has changed, but for the moment there is little reason why management should constrain themselves with compulsory arbitration provisions. Industrial action is constrained by law, by union rules and by the industrial climate. At the time of writing arbitration provisions exist in only a handful of trusts, one being reported as having introduced pendulum arbitration (NHSME, 1993). It has also been decided that the outstanding clinical grading appeals will be settled by a panel with chairpersons having the right to arbitrate failures to agree. The chairpersons have been nominated by ACAS.

The ACAS *Annual Report 1993* (1994:52) has a section which describes a situation which sums up many of the issues described in this chapter:

> Management at a newly formed trust in the West Country agreed with local trade union officials that a new consultative committee should

be formed to represent trust employees. A dispute arose over who should be represented on the committee. Following a collective conciliation meeting, it was agreed that the best way to explore recognition and negotiation problems was through a joint working party chaired by ACAS.

As a result of discussions, a single table collective bargaining arrangement was accepted by all the recognised trade unions. Agreement was also reached on the inclusion of an arbitration clause in the negotiating procedures and on who should represent trust employees at meetings.

*Pay, Job Evaluation and the Organisation of Work*

It has aready been suggested that local determination of a range of issues existed. Some of this is negotiated, some unilaterally determined by management. Considerable reorganisation of work patterns has taken place in many trusts. The NHSME (1993:11) states:

> No one will be surprised to learn that the most active practitioners of the introduction of local terms and conditions and pay spines are Ambulance Trusts. Of the 8 units that reported that they have comprehensive local pay and reward schemes including single pay spines, 4 were Ambulance services...A further 6 have introduced staff benefit packages/schemes and 11 are moving positively towards completely new, local pay systems.

This evidence was taken from the 44 per cent of units responding to a survey of 154 trusts. HCAs undertaking NVQs at Level 3 were reported by 80 per cent of respondents. Skill mix analyses were widespread and one health transport trust reported job reductions of 20 per cent. The average number of staff employed by trusts was 2303 with an average whole time equivalent (WTE) of 1817. The range of size was from 200 to 5000. Some 39 per cent of employees were part-time, accounting for 25 per cent of WTEs.

In many trusts new staff are employed on individual terms and conditions. Nursing and midwifery staff tend to be employed on pay related to the clinical grading, but the grade mix is being diluted in response to restructuring and natural wastage. Additional payments for such things as on-call or unsocial hours are being removed; ancillary staff bonus payments are being reduced and phased out. High grade staff often work on the bank at lower grades, F and G; grade nurses work additional hours at E grade. This is equivalent to working overtime at lower rates of pay, rather than at premium rates. What the evidence suggests is that although there is little sign of radical rearrangement of basic pay, terms and negotiating machinery, a lot of change in working patterns and arrangements is taking place.

Trusts are being encouraged by the NHSE to foster performance-related pay (PRP). This is also being promoted by the pay review bodies. So far PRP has tended to be confined to senior managers. There is a long history of PRP and a considerable literature on it pointing to the difficulties of designing performance targets, maintaining schemes and actually securing motivation. Performance schemes can be used to achieve organisational and cultural change, placing emphasis on performance and individualism. In the longer run they can create dissatisfaction where individuals begin to perceive the allocation of differential rewards as unfair. Trust remuneration committees are often faced with the dilemma of whether or not to award different PRP levels to executives who are part of what is seen to be a hard-working team. Paying everybody the same appears to contradict the principle. Making differential payments can undermine team spirit.

Derby City General Hospital Trust has proposed a form of PRP for its nursing and midwifery staff based on what it calls 'Professional Contribution Rating' (PCR). Such staff are placed on a pay spine, or assimilitated to it. Incremental steps on the pay spine are equivalent to 2 per cent. PCR can determine up to three steps in the lowest bar, two in the middle and one in the third. PCR is rated according to such criteria as personal effectiveness; interpersonal understanding; thinking and judgement; communication and teamwork. These criteria are related to behavioural characteristics and not explicitly to targets. Evaluation requires considerable qualitative judgement. There is a right of appeal against an assessment. The exercise has incorporated a new job evaluation system for nurses and midwives.

Job evaluation is widespread in the NHS. The clinical grading review, already referred to, graded all midwives, nurses and health visitors on the same scheme. The same criteria were used to fit job descriptions into a rank order of jobs. In job evaluation, criteria relate to such factors as the degree of experience required, judgement, managerial and supervisory responsibility and so on. The greater the content of a job in terms of such factors, the greater the score it receives and the higher the grade it falls into and, ultimately, the higher the pay awarded to it. The purpose of such schemes is to establish an agreed rationale for differentials, to try to make those affected feel that the differentials are fair because they relate to agreed criteria. Considerable dissatisfaction was generated by the manner in which the scheme was introduced, and this is reflected in the large number of appeals *it* generated. It is also a job classification scheme, which means that it might not be accepted as a defence against equal value claims. In spite of these drawbacks the scheme is still widely used. Evidence indicates that there are wide variations in grade mix on a regional basis. This suggests that, although the scheme is a national one, local labour market conditions can influence the distribution of grades between higher and lower. Although such variations suggest flexibility, this could be at the expense of national standards of care.

As indicated above, local schemes are being introduced, but not as rapidly as suggested by early statements from trusts. Local schemes have been proposed which are designed to incorporate all staff, but opposition from the BMA has made this difficult. The slow establishment of local schemes could reflect a number of factors. Job evaluation is expensive to introduce in terms of management and staff time and implementation costs. Existing schemes are still usable, and have a degree of flexibility. Management time and effort are locked into coping with the internal market and changes emanating from that. Job evaluation can reduce flexibility by tying staff into job descriptions and so on.

In our trust, management are using Whitley and the pay review bodies for annual awards. Existing job evaluation schemes have been retained with an amended appeals procedure, which allows for independent arbitration. Required restructuring is being achieved by skill mix reviews, and shift patterns are being reorganised by the staff themselves.

## Summary

This chapter has been concerned with indicating what might be meant by workplace industrial relations in a trust. The main pressures are external ones relating to costs and productivity demands. These are not greatly challenging the existing recognition arrangements or relations with trade unions. To the extent that our trust is typical, the response has been pragmatic. Where the future is so uncertain, the tendency is to modify the past rather than to try to plan wholesale change in this area. This response is as strategic as any available.

Chapter 10 illustrates some of the workplace issues arising from devolved bargaining by the use of case studies. Chapter 11 raises some of the more general issues linked to pay.

# 5

# Health and Safety at Work

NHS trusts are governed by common law duties and statute in respect of health and safety in the same way that other areas of employment are covered. Like these other areas of employment, the NHS also has its own special problems related to the kinds of work performed and the environment within which such work takes place. For example, approximately 25 per cent of all accidents reported to the Health and Safety Executive (HSE) are associated with manual handling. In the NHS, such accidents constitute 50 per cent of the total.

The NHS is responsible for providing health care and for the prevention of health problems. Health and safety at work in the NHS thus takes on additional dimensions. Patients, often referred to as customers, live for periods of time in what is the working environment of the staff. The NHS is itself a source of expertise with regard to health and safety matters. These factors interact to ensure a high profile for health and safety matters. Another way of putting this is that the risks associated with health and safety in the NHS are high for the employer. Failures can incur high costs, with patients, visitors and staff all being at risk. Staff are also at risk from patients, visitors and an environment trying to contain diseases, incorporating many dangerous substances and dangerous equipment. Patients are inevitably more vulnerable to health and safety hazards because of their conditions.

In spite of all of this, the analysis of health and safety as a factor contributing to production boils down to roughly the same abstract equation which applies everywhere. There is an optimum level of health and safety provision determined by costs and benefits. This is a complicated equation: costs and benefits are both hard to define and, where defined, difficult to measure. Also costs and benefits are unevenly distributed. Nevertheless, where limited budgets exist, priorities have to be established. Budgets also apply over time as well as in quantity. Achieving annual targets on budgets will lead to different priorities being established from those of budgets determined over longer periods: short-run gains may be given priority over longer-term gains. Trust strategic planning has to take careful account of health and safety issues.

The main statute in the UK covering this topic is The Health and Safety etc at Work Act (HSWA) 1974. A central provision of this Act is that 'an employer must ensure, so far as is reasonably practicable, the health, safety and welfare of all his employees while they are at work'. What the expression 'reasonably practicable' means is that some assessment has to be made of the scale and consequences of a risk compared with the time, trouble and cost of removing it. This is inevitable, but risk assessment will vary over time. Health and safety is inevitably a distributive matter and what we find in practice is that the two elements are unevenly distributed. What follows from this is that what is healthy or safe inevitably involves negotiation between employers and employees: health and safety cost money.

Historically employees have been willing to trade risk against higher pay from the employer gained from avoiding the financial costs of removing hazards. Employers have been willing to offer such inducements, and have lobbied the government to remove regulation. Part of the philosophy of the HSWA was to create self regulation of health and safety by the parties. History works against such a philosophy. Bayer (1988:74) in a historical survey of health and safety in three industries, tells us: 'Rather than a "discover and control" model of professional intervention, it would be more accurate in the coal industry to speak of a "disaster and response" model.' It could be argued that the response by the NHS to recent child murders in a Nottingham unit was an example of such an approach. Such events illustrate the point that health and safety cannot simply be left to the parties. There need to be external controls and pressures. Bayer also points to the 'heroic model' of 'whistleblowing'. Disclosing information on health and safety matters exposes individuals to punitive action by employers. This has never been an adequate way forward, although TURERA 1993, s. 28, now offers additional protection to employees faced with disciplinary action as a result of exposing or taking action to avoid dangers in the workplace.

There is another factor which creates pressure for external intervention. To the extent that health and safety provision incurs costs, failure to make such provision can give short-run competitive advantage in the market-place. Not surprisingly, the European Union (EU) is concerned to prevent such advantages being gained in this way. Consequently the EU is a major source of health and safety regulation for member states. There are also two United Nations bodies which set health and safety standards. The International Labour Organisation (ILO) has standards embodied in what are called conventions and recommendations. Similarly the World Health Organisation (WHO) also sets standards. These are not enforceable on member states to the extent that EU provisions are. Nevertheless they reflect worldwide concern over the issue of 'social dumping'. This is to do with the prevention of securing capital investment by offering investors lower costs deriving from such things as lower health and safety and environmental protection standards.

Implicit in the above is that legislation will only lay down minimum standards. These standards will take account of costs. Developing standards through the courts will be based on the shifting sands of the definition of what is 'reasonably practicable'. The standards set are also often vague. Trade unions are concerned about different standards because these can be used to play off sections of the membership against each other. At the place of work, trade unions can be seen to be one of the parties. From one place of work to another, both within and between countries, they can be seen as an external force trying to establish standards on behalf of members and preventing the kind of cost competition referred to above. TUC (1994) gives the following example:

> Concerns about unacceptable levels of pollution at a Danish pesticides plant led to its closure in the late 1980s. The firm responded by dismantling the plant and shipping it to Bradford, England. Soon production of the highly dangerous phenoxy pesticides (related to agent orange) had started in Britain, where environmental controls are less stringent.

The Danish trade union involved ensured that information was passed to the relevant union in the British plant. Trade unions liaise on an international basis in an attempt to control standards. No doubt the purchasers in the NHS will take account of health and safety matters in the allocation of their purchases between providers.

## The Legislative Framework

The main purpose of this chapter is to examine health and safety in the NHS. There is not space here to examine in detail the framework of legislation – there are plenty of accounts elsewhere. What follows is a brief outline. Within the UK the main statutory framework is provided by the HSWA 1974. The act established the Health and Safety Commission (HSC) with the overall duty of ensuring the proper enforcement of the act, the development of additional regulations, undertaking research, advising on codes of practice and so on. It is a tripartite body consisting of government, employer and trade union representatives. Sub-committees, similarly constituted, advise on specialist matters.

The work of the HSC is made operational by the Health and Safety Executive (HSE). Its staff are appointed by the HSC, subject to approval by the secretary of state. Employed by the HSE is an inspectorate with wide ranging powers. This inspectorate has rights of entry to premises, to examine work processes and substances and to seize and render harmless such substances and other articles. It can issue improvement and prohibition notices and initiate prosecutions. There are rights of appeal to the courts against its activities. Fines of up to £20000 for breaches of the HSWA can be enforced in the magistrates courts. The Crown Court can impose unlimited fines. In fact the courts can impose criminal law penalties and charges have included manslaughter. Civil claims for compensation may also be pursued. Penalties have tended to be low and the activities of the HSE have been hindered by inadequate funding in recent years (see Tombs, 1990). The difficulties of securing prosecutions, the weak results, and the above, have all combined to create concern about the effective implementation of the legislation in the UK.

The HSWA imposes general duties on employers and employees. Employers are expected to provide a healthy and safe working environment. In order to achieve this they are expected to ensure safe systems of work, a safe working environment, equipment designed to proper safety standards and properly maintained, and protection from harmful substances. They are also expected to provide information, training and statements of health and safety policy. Under the Reporting of Injuries, Diseases and Dangerous Occurrences Regulations (RIDDOR) 1985, employers are required to provide the HSE with records of accidents. The act imposes a duty on employees to take 'reasonable care' to avoid injury to themselves or others. Failure to do so could lead to disciplinary action or claims for negligence. Ultimate liability, however, lies with the employer. Professionals in the NHS have responsibilities in this area which derive from their codes of conduct and the regulatory bodies referred to in Chapter 3.

There is other legislation in the UK which affects the areas of health and safety. However, much more important now is the legislation of the EU. The Single European Act (SEA) signed in 1986 incorporated the new Article 118A into the Treaty of Rome. This has given the EU the power to impose health and safety legislation on member states via qualified majority voting. Since the article came into effect in 1988, a large number of directives has emanated from this source. An important development was the Control of Substances Hazardous to Health Regulations, (COSHH) 1988, implemented in 1989. These regulations have been applied in UK law. The COSHH regulations require what is called 'good working practice' to be applied to operations involving the use of hazardous substances. These involve risk assessment, exposure limits, testing of control equipment, health surveillance of employees and contractors, and the provision of training and information.

Probably the most important development since 1974 has been the introduction of the Management of Health and Safety at Work Regulations 1992 (MHSWR) together with an approved code of practice. These implemented the EU framework directive requiring detailed risk assessment of all hazards at work, along with requirements to take action, to train and to inform. Recent EU directives incorporated in UK law have covered such items as manual handling, the use of VDUs, use of work equipment and so on.

As suggested above, the EU has become the main driving force behind health and safety provision within member states. The period 1988–93 marked the EU's third action programme in this area. The years 1994-2000 will constitute the period of its fourth action programme. It is concerned to consolidate, and ensure enforcement of, existing legislation and to promote its health and safety agenda in non-member countries. There is the intention to examine the problems of specific groups, such as young people and the self-employed.

### Employee Involvement

The HSWA and the safety representatives and Safety Committees Regulations 1978 gave certain rights to recognized independent trade unions in respect of their involvement in health and safety at the place of work. There is no provision for statutory recognition of trade unions in the UK. This focus on trade unions reflects their wishes and influence in a period when they were much stronger. Unions have traditionally argued that wider representation of employees would work to undermine their influence. Similarly some unions have believed that representation on health and safety matters is not easily separated from other issues. Health and safety is a traditional grievance area and issues arising in this area overlap general terms and conditions issues. For this reason it has sometimes been the case that shop stewards have undertaken the role of health and safety representation along with their other duties. This approach is reinforced by the belief that health and safety is often channelled along the lines of consultation rather than negotiation. In the NHS the traditional approach from all the unions has been to appoint separate health and safety representatives.

The legislation allows recognised independent trade unions to appoint health and safety representatives. Such representatives have legal rights. They have the right to carry out the following functions: to investigate potential hazards, dangerous occurrences and the causes of accidents; to investigate employee complaints about health and safety; to make representations to management; to represent employees in discussions with the HSE and its inspectors and to carry out routine inspections of the place of work. To help them carry out these functions they have the right to require the employer to establish a health and safety committee, the right to time off to perform their functions and the right to time off for training in health and safety and the effective performance of their functions; they also have rights to information. The legislation imposes no duties on such representatives. Although appointed, their activities are voluntary. Their effectiveness is very much constrained by the attitudes of employers. Although TURERA 1993 has introduced some additional protection for health and safety representatives, their effectiveness still depends very much upon the willingness of employers to recognise their contribution. In fact, as indicated above, their right to exist depends upon trade union recognition by the employer.

The decline in trade union membership and recognition in general has weakened such representation. No doubt EU policy will push the UK towards employee representation to ensure adequate involvement. Evidence in Europe suggests that where trade unions exist they will continue to dominate representation. As indicated in Chapter 3, some of the membership trends in the NHS have been contrary to those in general. Health and safety representation and committees still flourish in the NHS. Given the pressures on costs, health and safety is becoming a growing priority for employees in the NHS. Professionals have to be doubly cautious in view of the threats to their right to practise where they act unsafely according to their responsibilities as practitioners in their own right.

## Health and Safety at Trust Level

*Policy*

Our trust, as required by law, has a Health and Safety at Work policy. The scope of the policy is expressed in the following terms:

> The policy applies to all employees of the Trust, including non-executive directors and 'bank' staff. In addition, the Trust will take all reasonably practicable steps to ensure a safe environment for those employees engaged in contracts for services, volunteers and hospital visitors.

Ultimate responsibility for the policy rests with the chief executive of the trust. On a day-by-day basis, this is delegated. The director of personnel is responsible for acting as the initial point of contact with the HSE and its inspectorate, ascertaining their requirements and referring them to the appropriate director or departmental head. Personnel is also responsible for organising training programmes to meet the requirements of legislation; maintaining records of accidents, establishing reporting and investigation procedures; attending safety committee meetings as an ex-officio member; and maintaining a register of safety representatives and safety committee members and their areas of activities. The personnel director also has a co-ordinating role overseeing all matters of health and safety and is expected to report to the board of the trust on such matters. This also incorporates notifying and advising on changes in the law.

The director of facilities has responsibilities related to estates and facilities – these incorporate buildings and equipment. This is a very wide remit which involves advice on health and safety legislation as it affects existing and new buildings, security and alarm systems, fire precautions, safe installation and maintenance of all equipment and so on. The director liaises directly with the HSE and local planning and licensing authorities, maintains a register of competent inspection staff and is responsible for risk assessment.

The occupational health services manager has the responsibility of identifying hazards and dangerous working practices. There is also a responsibility for pre-employment health screening and identifying staff potentially at risk. The policy also tells us that this manager has a duty to: 'Provide advice to the Trust, managers and staff in relation to current health and safety legislation, eg. Manual Handling Operations Regulations, 1992, Display Screen Equipment Regulations, 1992.' The occupational health team is expected to provide training in risk assessment and ergonomics, and in first aid at work. Records of accidents to staff and occupational health records are expected to be maintained, and reports made to appropriate committees. Section 41 of the General Whitley Council Agreement lays down guidelines for the activities of occupational health services at the place of work.

Managers in general are given the responsibility for ensuring that their staff are properly inducted and trained, and to carry out 12-monthly safety audits of their areas of control. Similarly individual employees are reminded of their duty of care. The policy also recognises the rights of safety representatives to time off with pay, and to the protection of pay of staff unable to work as a result of a HSE order. Essentially the policy statement is an outline of the duties of the trust under health and safety legislation. It also indicates where responsibility lies and there-fore the process of accountability. Line managers have day-to-day responsibilities, channelled upwards through line directors, to whom they are accountable, and overseen by the director of personnel.

Policy development is aided by monthly meetings of a health and safety review group which is made up of managers. This includes the personnel director, facilities director, occupational health manager and managers from different specialisms. This provides a forum for ensuring both development and integration of policy in the light of changing legislation, reports of the trust health and safety committee and the information gathered from reporting of hazards, substances and accidents and dangerous occurrences. At the time of writing this committee was also responding to a HSE inquiry into the implementation of the COSHH regulations in the NHS region. The HSE had expressed reservations about the uneven implementation of the COSHH regulations in units in the region. The NHSE had instructed trusts to examine and report on their practice.

*Trust Health and Safety Committee*

Our trust has a health and safety committee made up of joint management/staff membership. It consists of nine staff members and seven management members. The staff members are safety representatives of recognised trade unions. The overall objective of the committee is: 'Promotion of co-operation between the Trust management and employeees in instigating and developing and carrying out measures to ensure the health and safety of its employees.' Its main functions, as listed in its constitution, consist of an overview of all health and safety matters. The committee meets twice a year, can establish sub-committees and can co-opt members.

The committee appoints a chairman from the management

side and a vice-chairman from the staff side annually. This reflects its status as a consultative committee, although the staff side are allowed a pre-meeting, where they meet separately and discuss the agenda in advance. The committee is a forum for discussing issues rather than raising grievances related to health and safety. Recent agenda contain COSHH discussions as a standard item. Car parking and the safety of provision is another standard item. Similarly the protection of staff in the community recurs. There is no doubt that the committee provides a useful forum for staff and managers. It communicates both parties' concerns, and these are encapsulated in an annual report to the trust board. Such issues inform the management health and safety action plan.

*Health Service Hazards*

The health and safety action plan for the trust contains over 40 items. These items give an indication of the nature of health and safety problems in the NHS. Some have already been referred to. What follows is a selection from the list of items. Each item is allocated to a member of the management team.

Bomb alert, Personal Protective Equipment Regulations, 1992, and abrasive wheels regulations are general to industry. HSE Guidance HS(G) 70, Control of Legionellosis, has important implications in the NHS. This could be seen as a disaster/response intervention consequent on the outbreak of Legionnaire's Disease at Stafford Hospital in the 1980s. Disposal of clinical waste, hepatitis B and Sharps policies are all related. These policies are designed to protect staff from threats arising from dangerous materials. Protection of staff working in the community is of considerable importance in the NHS. Midwives have a duty to visit, for example. This duty can lead them into dangerous inner city areas or households. Should they have the right to be accompanied and, if so, by whom? Research at Keele University shows that midwives often ask their husbands to accompany them on late night visits to dangerous areas. Ambulance staff and mental health staff all have duties in the community. Household hazards range from dangerous premises and persons to dangerous animals and insects.

Other hazards include radiation. The Food Safety Act 1990 is of considerable importance in the NHS. Both these areas require policies. Violence to staff and stress-related illnesses are both growing phenomena, and the trust has developed policies in these areas. Rapid change induces stress and this leads to an emphasis on the symptoms of stress and its management, rather than ameliorating the causes. Smoking policies at the place of work have developed throughout industry. Given the nature of the NHS, such policies present special difficulties. Passive smoking is a well established health hazard and the NHS has obvious responsibilities in this area. Special difficulties arise not only from staff who smoke, but also from visitors and patients. Many are in extremely stressful situations and regard smoking as relieving stress. Mental health units also have special problems in this area. Establishing complete no-smoking policies becomes difficult. Can smoking be confined to medical prescription?

Our trust has a no smoking policy. This refers to the HSWA requirement on employers to ensure so far as is reasonably practicable the health, safety and welfare of all employees. It also refers to a WHO resolution of 1986 which urged employers to implement smoking control strategies to ensure the protection of non-smokers from involuntary exposure to tobacco smoke. The UK government strategy *The Health of the Nation* (DOH, 1992b) stated that the NHS should develop an exemplary role in making a smoke-free environment the norm; this is also referred to in the policy:

> No smoking by staff, patient, relatives and visitors on the premises of the Trust. Exceptionally in a clinical area, where a patient or relative is severely distressed by the restriction, the Nurse in Charge shall treat the individual with consideration and make short-term arrangements to deal sensitively with the situation.

Mentally ill patients are excluded from the ban, but their staff, visitors and relatives are not. Breach of the policy constitutes serious misconduct.

The trust also has a policy on alcohol-related problems. It points to the costs of alcohol-related absenteeism and alcohol-impaired work. Reference is made to the fact that most of the occupations with a higher than average association with problem drinking can be found in the NHS: doctors, financial agents, catering staff, cooks, electrical engineers and service workers, and so on. Staff are not allowed to drink during working hours, except on very special occasions authorised by management. The policy document is 14 pages long. It contains advice on identifying alcohol-related problems and how to deal with these, outlining the services available for counselling and treatment. The responsibilities of managers, staff and trade union representatives are identified.

Following the EU Regulations 1992, already referred to, the trust has appropriately amended policies on manual handling operations and display screen equipment. There is also a first aid policy. 'Hepatitis B and Employment' is another important policy document, designed to ensure protection and control. All of these policy documents contain elaborate provision, in terms of definitions, risk assessment, allocation of responsibilities and training requirements. They all involve considerable cost in terms of human and other resources.

### Occupational Health and Welfare

All of the above overlaps into what can be described as occupational health and welfare. It was stated above that health and safety provision was expensive. Nichol (1994) tells us: 'Every year the National Health Service loses output equivalent to the work of nearly 10,000 full-time staff through medically certificated mental illness. Any reduction in this could increase output correspondingly.' This quotation draws attention to two points. Health and safety provision which prevents accidents and illness saves on absenteeism costs. It also makes workers more effective. The second point is that attention should be paid to the needs of individuals. Home and work are environments which interact and both can be sources of stress. Occupational health provision, for which the NHS is very well equipped, should include identification of personal problems whatever the source of these.

The trust has an occupational health department which contracts to provide a range of services to the trust. Many of these are directly associated with the policies referred to above. Probably its most important role is that of screening potential employees and ensuring that they, and existing employees are fit for work and that it does not become detrimental to them. The department has a responsibility to identify hazards, as referred to earlier, and to use its expertise to control these. It also plays a large part in designing the various policies referred to above. An obvious provision of occupational health would be to make available professional counselling. Our trust has established sub-groups to implement the NHS Health at Work Initiative – often described in the literature as equivalent to a 'positive health programme'. One of these is the positive mental health sub-group. A stress questionnaire was issued to all staff and analysed by the medical audit team. Stress management courses were introduced, and access to a confidential counselling service with referrals or 'open door' access to another, therefore independent, trust made available. Smoking cessation sessions were made available to supplement the no-smoking policy.

A sub-group was established to promote 'healthy eating' and another to promote 'sensible drinking' and to support staff with drink problems. Another group promotes physical fitness by laying on fitness classes, fitex testing, providing prescriptions for swimming, creating events involving exercise and seeking staff discounts from fitness clubs. Positive attitudes towards sex and sexuality and developing appropriate HIV/AIDS policies are also part of the agenda. In its 1994/5 service agreement the occupational health department committed itself to additional health screening provision, subsidised aromatherapy and chiropody services and extended counselling provision.

Promoting the welfare of the employee in these generalised ways is not new. Counselling has always been associated with the development of personnel policies. Many companies provided a whole range of facilities for employees: social clubs, gymnasia, football, cricket and athletics facilities, drama societies, convalescent homes and so on. Some were very much concerned with the moral welfare of their employees. Many of these provisions were taken over by local authorities, and in recent years have been privatised. There is some indication that employers are reinvesting in some of these facilities, a revival of what used to be called 'welfare capitalism'. Establishing such facilities is a way of securing commitment. Access to private health care is a 'perk' for many employees. The equivalent in our trust is 'fast access to health care', with employees securing priority provision – raising the prospect of yet another tier of health provision. On the other hand, it could be regarded as a form of staff discount, or something equivalent to a substitute for a share allocation.

## Conclusion

Legislation imposes costs on employers in respect of health and safety. The subject is very much seen as part of the human resourcing division within the field of HRM. It is also, because of these costs, and the potential benefits, part of strategic planning. The whole area needs to be linked to corporate plans, and the earlier references to social dumping indicated that location of production could be a factor in investment decisions related to relevant health, safety and environmental legislation.

NHS units do not have the flexibility which units in other industries have. We have also seen that the nature of its product, and its system of production, imposes specific requirements on the NHS in these areas. These requirements are manifested at trust level. Similarly the product generates a labour force with skills relevant to the needs of health, safety and welfare. All of this is reflected in the extent and nature of the provision: the employer in the NHS has on hand resources which are not available to other employers.

The work of NHS employees exposes them to a unique combination of hazards. Their expertise also makes them more demanding. Nevertheless this expertise does not guarantee full protection against risks, carelessness and the consequences of excessive working hours. The NHS is faced by considerable pressures from reorganisation and the attempt to save on costs. At the same time there is an increase in litigation combined with greater exposure to public scrutiny, and a Patients' Charter which encourages both. The EU regulations of 1992 are of considerable importance in the NHS, particularly the manual handling regulations. Professional staff in the NHS face greater personal consequences where unsafe practices lead to their negligent performance. Considerations following from this are often brought forward in discussions of junior doctors' hours of work, for example. A complication for the management of health and safety in the NHS is that these professionals are arbiters of safe practice, and have codes of conduct which require them to be so.

As stated at the beginning of this chapter, the objective has been to give the flavour of health, safety and welfare provision in the NHS and not a comprehensive guide to legislation, regulations and codes of practice, whether emanating from the state or from the professional bodies themselves. The health and welfare of employees are not solely the product of the background of provision focused on in this chapter. All aspects of the employment relationship are relevant. For example, hours of work, staffing ratios, skill mix, sick pay and so on impinge on health and safety. The nature of clinical and medical care is such that stress-related illnesses are bound to be of some importance. Nursing staff tend to have high sickness rates which can be related to the nature and intensity of the work undertaken.

# 6

# Equal Opportunities

The purpose of this chapter is to raise the main issues associated with the concept of equal opportunities, to locate these in the NHS at national level, and then to examine policy and practice at the level of the trust. In the logic of economic theory it does not make sense for employers to discriminate in recruitment, or in any other way, against employees on grounds which are not related to the job for which they are sought or for which they are employed. To do so is to limit the supply of labour available, and this, other things being equal, will make wages higher. It would follow from this that there may be some motivation for those in employment to restrict entry into that employment.

Economists do take account of prejudice. Both employers and employees may assert such prejudice. From the point of view of the individual discriminated against, the source of such discrimination makes little difference. What this model would suggest is that employees are likely to create obstacles for employers who try to enlarge their sources of recruitment. Employees in managerial posts may have a vested interest in restricting competition for such posts. Trade union representatives may seek to protect the position of current members.

Discrimination might persist for other reasons. Equal opportunities policies and strategies require investment. For example, the introduction of creche facilities costs money in the short run which may not be recouped in that period. Managers on annual budget targets might prefer to postpone or neglect such investments. Another factor reinforcing discrimination is the already unequal distribution of training and education which works to the detriment of females and ethnic minority groups, not to mention people from low income and deprived backgrounds. Selecting on the basis of acquired skill levels and education will simply reinforce the existing inequality in these areas.

The difficulty with separating equal opportunities as an issue is that this fails to take account of the fact that the system of production as a whole inevitably works against equality of treatment. What this serves to explain is why initiatives in this area have not produced more radical change in the distribution of job opportunities for those discriminated against on the grounds of sex, race and disability. These are the grounds for discrimination on which legislative action has tended to focus. That there are other grounds for discrimination which might be regarded as unacceptable hardly requires comment. One consequence of legislation is that it imposes potential costs on employers and these affect economic considerations. The same is true of any damage to the image of the enterprise arising from bad publicity.

This chapter is concerned with the NHS as a case study in the area of equal opportunity. There are explicitly stated policies at both national and local level, and these can be examined in terms of their stated objectives and, to some extent, achievements. For a broder examination of the issues the reader is advised to see Dickens (1994:253–96).

### Legislative Background

The equal opportunities policy of our trust contains an appendix which summarises legislation. This indicates what an employer considers to be the most relevant legislation in this field and provides us with a brief guide to it. The trust's equal opportunities policy takes account of relevant acts of Parliament, as follows:

1. **Sex Discrimination Act 1975** (and its **Amendments 1986**) – this act makes it unlawful to discriminate directly or indirectly (see Section 5) on the grounds of sex or marital status or to apply requirements or conditions which have a disproportionately disadvantageous effect on people of a particular sex or marital status where these cannot be justified. It also applies to discriminatory employment advertising and makes it unlawful to apply pressure to discriminate or to aid discrimination by another person.

2. **Race Relations Act 1976** – this act makes it unlawful to discriminate directly or indirectly on the grounds of colour, race, nationality (including citizenship) or ethnic or national origin, or to apply requirements or conditions which have a disproportionately disadvantageous effect on people of a particular racial group and which cannot be justified on non-racial grounds. It also applies to discriminatory employment advertising and makes it unlawful to apply pressure to discriminate or to aid discrimination by another person.

3. **Equal Pay Act 1970** (and its **Amendments 1984**) – this act established the right of women and men to equal treatment in relation to contractual terms and conditions of employment when they are employed on the same or broadly similar work or work of equal value.

4. **The Disabled Persons (Employment) Acts 1944 and 1958** – these acts make specific provision for the employment of people with disabilities. Under the provision of the quota scheme, employers with more than 20 staff have an obligation to employ at least 3 per cent registered disabled people. The legislation also imposes certain obligations on those firms which are below the quota when engaging employees or when discharging a registered disabled employee.

5. **The Chronically Sick and Disabled Persons Act** (and its **Amendments 1976**) – this legislation imposes obligations on employers to provide access to premises and facilities for people with disabilities.

6. **The Rehabilitation of Offenders Act 1974** (and **Exceptions Order 1975** and **Amendments 1986**) – this act provides that if a convicted person completes a specified period without being convicted of further offences the conviction can be regarded as 'spent'. These convictions then do not have to be revealed and may not be used as grounds for exclusion from employment or promotion. If the *work involves people who are directly receiving a health service,* then applicants must disclose any convictions they might have. Advice can be obtained from the director of personnel.

The above is a brief survey of the most important legislation in this area. Statutes will be referred to in the context of empirical analysis of some of the issues at NHS national and trust levels, and this will allow for some evaluation of the legislation's impact. For the future, the trust was planning to take account of the impact of the Disability Discrimination Act 1995.


**Issues in the NHS**

In 1990, the Equal Opportunities Commission (EOC) conducted a survey into women's employment in the NHS, see p. 141 (EOC, 1991). The EOC was set up under the 1975 Sex Discrimination Act (SDA 1975). It has duties to work towards the elimination of discrimination; to promote equality between men and women and to review the working of the SDA, 1975 and 1986, the Equal Pay Act 1970 (EPA 1970) and the 1983 Equal Value Amendment (EVA 1983). In order to carry out these duties it has the power to conduct investigations which must have terms of reference, to secure documents; to give evidence, to serve non-discrimination notices on employers prohibiting unlawful acts under the equality legislation above and to require an employer to take specific action to comply with the law. Employers have a right of appeal to an industrial tribunal.

The 1990 survey followed a formal investigation into the Southern Derbyshire Health Authority which had been instigated as a result of a complaint from a woman who had applied for employment and training as a midwife at Derby City Hospital. She claimed to have been refused at the time on the grounds that she had pre-school children. After thorough investigation, a non-discrimination notice was issued against the Health Authority. The notice identified breaches of sections of the SDA 1975. For example, the requirement that applicants do not have children of pre-school age indirectly discriminated against married women because the proportion of those who could comply with it was considerably smaller than within the unmarried female group. The Authority was required to furnish the EOC with a commitment to abandon the practice, and to provide information into the future to allow the situation to be monitored.

One response of the NHSE (then the NHSME) was to commission the Office of Public Management to report on equal opportunities in the NHS and to try to establish a programme of action. (*NHSE*, 1991). The NHSME was also aware that it was being studied by the EOC. To the EOC, the NHS was important because its employees were state employees, and thus covered by the then EC legislation. Also the NHS was the largest employer of women in Western Europe. The report identified a number of indications of gender discrimination:

> 79% of employees were female and concentrated in four occupational groupings: nursing and midwifery – 90% female; professions allied to medicine – 88% female; administrative and clerical – 84% female; and ancillary staff – 74% female.

> doctors – 26% female; ambulance staff – 21% female; works' staff – 7% female; and maintenance staff – 5% female.

The report found women to be employed on a part-time basis in much greater proportion than men; wide pay differences between the sexes, in favour of men; longer periods for women to secure higher grades and so on. Most of these findings were derived from secondary sources rather than from the survey itself which focused on the existence and content of policies and their monitoring. Perhaps the main significance of the report was that it provided a rationale for NHSE strategy in this area. On page 18 of the report we are told: 'This report demonstrates that high labour turnover and staff shortages are the inevitable consequence of the failure of the NHS to address issues of sex and marital discrimination, and to promote good quality equal opportunities employment policies.' Other things being equal, there was no doubt truth in this comment. However, the continuing recession and growing NHS redundancies have mitigated the staff shortage situation and no doubt undermined some of the equal opportunity policies. The report did give detailed advice to the NHSE on how to develop a strategy for equal opportunities. It also turned equal opportunities into an important 'image' issue for the NHS in a period of significant change. The NHS had to be seen to respond.

The NHS is an Opportunity 2000 employer. The associated campaign was launched in 1991 by Business in the Community with the objective of increasing the quality and quantity of female employment. Organisations representing five million employees are now signed up to this project. In 1992, the NHSE set itself eight objectives under this iniative (DOH, 1992a).

1   To increase the number of women in general management posts from 18% in 1991 to 30% in 1994.
2   Increase the number of qualified women accountants in the NHS.
3   Increase the percentage of women consultants from 15.5% in 1991 to 20% by 1994.
4   Increase representation of women as members of Trusts and Authorities from 29.9% in 1991 to 35% in 1994.
5   Introduce a programme allowing women aspiring to management positions to go through a development centre.
6   Introduce initiatives on recruitment and retention to ensure that the number of qualified nurses and midwives leaving the profession does not rise.
7   Ensure that following maternity leave or a career break all women, including those returning to nursing part-time or as a job-share, are able to return at a grade commensurate with their leaving grade and to work of a similar status.
8   Monitor the time taken for nurses to reach management positions to ensure that men and women have equal access to these positions.

At trust level these objectives are transformed into an action plan consisting of key tasks with dates for implementation. For example, 28 February was given as the date for adoption of Opportunity 2000 as part of the trust's strategic management objectives. The targets of 40 per cent of accountants in post being female and 20 per cent of consultants had been achieved before the end of 1992. Incorporating PRP targets for senior managers was established on 31 April 1993. In fact, all of the Opportunity 2000 objectives had been incorporated into practice by early 1994.

All of the above was under the control of the personnel director and represents the influence of personnel, or HRM, on strategy at both national and local level. The process also illustrates, via the influence of the EOC, the impact of legislation. Whatever the motivation of the NHSE and the trust board, positive action was taken at the place of work to ensure better opportunities for women.

## Opportunities for Ethnic Minorities

In December 1993, the secretary of state introduced *Ethnic Minority Staff in the NHS: A Programme of Action*, (NHSME, 1993b). Part of the background to this was the work of the King's Fund Task Force which spent 1986 to 1990 examining issues of racial equality in the NHS. In its final report (King's Fund, 1991), the task force noted the need for equal opportunities objectives in the area of race to become a formal part of the duties of NHS managers. The *Programme of Action* addressed this recommendation. The overall aim of the programme was stated to be: 'To achieve the equitable representation of minority ethnic groups at all levels in the NHS (including professional staff groups), reflecting the ethnic composition of the local population.' In the document there is a comment on the terminology:

> The term 'ethnic minority', or more precisely 'people from a minority (ethnic) group' has been used throughout. Whilst it is appreciated that people from minority white groups (e.g. Irish, Polish) may experience discrimination in employment, the programme is mainly intended to address the pressing need for equality of opportunity in employment of black and minority ethnic people.

Prior to the publication of this programme, the NHS had already been committed to the central collection of ethnic monitoring data. This was to be achieved for senior managers, nursing and midwifery staff by Autumn 1994. Data for remaining staff would follow in 1995. The ethnic classifications would be those used in the Census, as recommended by the Commission for Racial Equality (CRE). It is also stated in the programme that its goals are broadly in line with that Commission's Code of Practice (1982).

The CRE was set up under the Race Relations Act 1976. Its duties and powers are very similar to those of the EOC: to work towards the elimination of discrimination, to promote equality of opportunity and to advise the secretary of state on legislation. It also has powers of investigation and can issue and enforce non-discrimination notices. The eight goals of the programme of action cover the range of HRM activities:

Recruitment and Selection.
NHS Trusts and health authorities to include in their business plans a local objective to increase the proportion of minority ethnic staff in areas and grades where they are under-represented, within a specified timescale, until fair representation is achieved.

Staff Development
To maximise the skills and potential of all personnel in a multi-racial NHS workforce, with particular emphasis on the identifiable needs of people from minority ethnic groups.

Racial Harassment
To ensure NHS workplaces are free from harassment and discrimination, including racial harassment.

Appointments to NHS Boards
To increase the number of black and ethnic minority Chairs of NHS authorities and Trusts, and Community Health Councillors, to reflect the composition of the population served.

Service Delivery
To provide a better service to patients by optimal use of the workforce.

Doctors
To ensure that the time spent in higher specialist training by doctors with right of residence from minority ethnic groups equates to the time spent in higher specialist training by white doctors with right of residence.

Nurses
NHS authorities and Trusts to set a local objective to achieve equitable representation of ethnic minority nurses at G grade (ward manager or community equivalent) within five years. Progress towards achieving this objective should be reviewed annually as part of the business planning cycle.

Management Training Schemes
(A) RHAs and the NHS Management Training Scheme to take steps to increase each year to a locally determined level the proportion of minority ethnic applicants for the NHS Management Training Scheme, and the proportion obtaining a place on the Scheme. This will require the elimination of bias and in some instances positive action in recruitment, selection and training processes.
(B) A similar requirement is placed on RHAs in respect of the NHS Finance Training Scheme and other career grade training schemes, and on NHS organisations below RHA level where there are locally managed training and development schemes.

The above agenda illustrates the role of the NHSE in HRM at national level. Trusts are bound to respond to a costly exercise and are instructed to incorporate the policies in business plans. Under each of the goals the programme lays down ideas for achieving them. There is advice on advertising and recruitment methods: for example, they are advised to advertise in ethnic minority media, to promote a positive multicultural image, to insert positive action messages, referring to the relevant section of the Race Relations Act, and so on. The training of all staff on selection panels is particularly emphasised.

## General Whitley Council Provisions

The General Whitley Council has also reached agreement on various aspects of discrimination, and this provides additional central direction. In early 1994, the secretary of state accepted *Equal Opportunities: An Enabling Agreement on Recruitment and Selection Procedures* as section 13 of The General Whitley Council Handbook. This incorporates most of the Programme of Action and the EOC Report recommendations as part of conditions of service.

The General Whitley Council Conditions also deal with other aspects of equal opportunities. Section 7 adds age, religion and creed, and sexual orientation to race, sex, disability and marital status as forbidden grounds for discrimination. Section 8 asserts the unacceptability of harassment at work in general, but also specifically links it to the characteristics of employees referred to in section 7. It recommends the separate statement of a policy on harassment and the procedures for dealing with it. Section 9 of Whitley deals with Child Care and commends

> the establishing of an appropriate range of facilities to assist with child care including workplace nurseries, creches, holiday and after school playschemes. In addition, it believes that each health authority should consider other forms of child care facilities which may be appropriate, e.g. child care allowances, a voucher arrangement which would enable health authorities to contribute directly towards the cost of an employee's child care arrangements or any similar or appropriate arrangement.

This, of course, is largely exhortatory, but it does point to ways of helping those with the responsibility of caring for children. Creche provision is fairly widespread, but our research has not provided evidence of the other facilities commended. Section 10 of Whitley deals with retainer schemes. It expresses the belief that health authorities should draw up such schemes, to allow career breaks of up to five years without breaking continuity of employment, although the period of the break itself would not be counted.

Section 11 of Whitley deals with job sharing. It defines job-sharing as 'a way of working where the duties and responsibilities of a post which would normally be held by one individual are shared'. This is designed to reinforce flexible employment practices which would allow greater access to work for people with caring commitments – generally women. The section suggests how such schemes should be best implemented to prevent the exploitation of job-sharers: two people employed to do one job part-time often end up doing more than one job. Problems of holiday pay and other entitlements are referred to with recommended solutions. Currently flexibility is leading to contracts which exclude such considerations. NHS staff on the bank (employed on an 'on call' basis) often get paid by the hour, and so on. Trends are working very much against the equal opportunities intentions of Whitley, both in the NHS and elsewhere.

Section 12 of Whitley also has links with equal opportunities. This section is concerned with special leave for domestic, personal and family reasons. This is an area which again especially affects women. Maternity provisions, as determined by UK and EU legislation, are well known, or easily referred to and therefore not detailed here. Section 12 incorporates paternity leave as a recommendation, along with leave for caring, not only for children, but for other close relatives or dependants. Adoption leave is also recommended in this section.

Whitley thus covers the range of measures associated with equal opportunities. Many trusts have, and will adopt, policies derived from Whitley. However, as indicated above, the reforms and economic pressures are working against many of the Whitley recommendations, and the continuation of Whitley itself.

## Equal Opportunities in our Trust

In our trust, equal opportunities monitoring started in 1991. The analysis for 1993 showed that 96 vacancies were processed with a total of 723 applications. 40 per cent of females were shortlisted as against 27 per cent male; ten males and 86 females were appointed; 39 per cent of white applicants and 19 per cent of non-white applicants were shortlisted; 14 per cent of white applicants and 5 per cent of non-whites were appointed; 39 per cent of single applicants were shortlisted and 15 per cent appointed; 36 per cent of married applicants were shortlisted and 13 per cent appointed.

Such statistics give a very limited view of the process of selection in terms of equal opportunities. More information would be needed on the jobs and the background of the applicants in terms of qualifications and experience. This information is available to the trust board through interrogation. The annual report offers some conclusions. There were seen to be no significant changes in the workforce profile since 1991. It was recorded that the trust was not attracting high levels of applications from ethnic minority groups or from the disabled. This was partly explained by reorganisation and the consequent emphasis on internal advertising and transfers. It was felt that external advertising should use a wider range of outlets, but the additional expense involved was also recognised. Internal reviews of recruitment and selection had concluded that there was no evidence of unlawful discrimination or bias.

The trust provides creche facilities; Jobshare opportunities and career breaks had been introduced. The annual report stated that there had been little take up of the latter two facilities, and suggested that this might be something to do with the recession.

*Equal Opportunities Policy*

The aim of the policy is stated to be: 'to ensure that no job applicant or employee receives less favourable treatment on the grounds of race, colour, nationality, ethnic origin, sex, marital status, sexual orientation, responsibility for dependants, age or disability.' The scope of the policy is designed to ensure high standards of employment practices in: advertising; recruitment and selection; promotion; transfer; performance review; training and development; disciplinary and grievance handling. It points to elements of indirect discrimination: a height requirement excludes more women than men; a requirement to wear skirts and not trousers might exclude ethnic minority females. The trust also undertakes to vary work requirements where reasonably practicable to accommodate religious and cultural needs.

Ultimate responsibility for the proper application of the policy rests with the trust board, with co-ordination and administration delegated to the personnel director. This includes training responsibilities, with such responsibilities including induction, and management and staff training in equal opportunities. Managers are made aware in the policy of their responsibilities in their areas of operation. The policy also provides for adevertising, recruitment and selection procedures. 'Wilful discrimination', on the grounds referred to in the aims of the policy, victimisation or harassment, of employees, clients or members of the general public, are deemed to be serious misconduct, which could lead to dismissal.

The policy also provides for monitoring and suggests that factual evidence for its ineffectiveness would include situations where the groups referred to in the aims:

> do not apply for employment or promotion, or fewer than might be expected apply
> are not shortlisted, recruited or promoted, or are not appointed, in ways which differ significantly from their proportions in applications
> are under-represented in certain sections, departments, grades and/or shifts.

As suggested earlier, the monitoring process could be further refined. Some groups may be over-represented in unpopular shifts, either at particular times or during holiday periods. Ethnic minority groups might be concentrated in late shifts; single people might be concentrated in Christmas working.

The trust has a harassment policy which is linked to its equal opportunities policy and the requirements of the General Whitley Council. Examples of harassment are given under the headings of sexual, racial, age and disability. Under sexual, apart from obvious examples, pin-ups and pornographic material are prohibited on the premises. Jokes relating to race, age and disability are given as an example of harassment. The procedure provides for informal and confidential discussions with staff who feel they are being harassed, and provides for disciplinary action where harassment is proved. This is always a difficult and sensitive area. The policy provides for awareness training for all staff. Attitudes have changed considerably in these areas, and such training is often more necessary with older, long-serving staff.

There is a retainer scheme, the purpose of which is to allow staff, with two years or more employment at the trust, to take a break from work to fulfil domestic commitments such as 'care for pre-school children, care for a dependant relative'. Such breaks are granted for up to two years. The scheme provides for periods back at work during the break to allow for updating and so on. The trust leave policy provides for carer, adoption and paternity leave. Carer leave is for up to five working days, with pay, with no more than ten in any 12-month period. It covers bereavement, illness of a child or dependant and breakdown of normal carer arrangements. Adoption leave grants time as necessary to complete formal adoptive procedures and up to six weeks when the child enters the adoptive parents' full-time care – all with pay. Paternity leave is for five working days with pay from the time of birth or within four weeks of it. EU provisions, opposed by the government in the UK, do not provide for paid paternity leave. The trust provides maternity leave in accordance with the provisions of the Whitley General Council Agreement.

Another policy connected with equal opportunities and designed to provide effective clinical care is the interpreters policy. This is directed at patients and places a responsibility on clinical staff to make use of the trust's register of interpreters. Three potential barriers to communication are identified: unable to speak and comprehend the English language; mute and/or cannot hear; blind. The switchboard supervisor has the responsibilty of keeping and maintaining the register to ensure that interpreters in African, Asian, European, Braille and sign languages are available. The above, related to interpreters, is also incorporated in the Patient's Charter.

## Conclusion

The purpose of this chapter has been to identify the main issues relating to equal opportunities within the NHS. It can be seen that there are policies at the centre, and many of these have been developed during a period of so-called 'decentralisation'. Given that this is a sensitive area, and given the singling out of the NHS by both the EOC and the CRE, 'image' factors no doubt play some part. This is also linked to the high degree of sensitivity of employees and the general public to the major changes taking place in the NHS. In this area it would appear that the NHSE is determined that the NHS be seen as a model employer. This is clearly beneficial to those who have any relationship with the NHS.

Examining the policies of our trust provides practical illustration of the impact of NHSE policies and legislation as they manifest themselves at the place of work. No attempt has been made to examine the legislation in any detailed form. The EU is now a driving force in the equal opportunities legislation of member states. Again this process has not been examined in any detail. Individual rights in this area are growing; so also are the penalties attached to infringement of these rights. The explicit strategy of the NHS and our trust makes provision which goes beyond legal minimum requirements, whatever their source. In practice, economic forces might overwhelm the explicit intent of such a strategy.

It is also hoped that this chapter has illustrated the very wide range of issues associated with the concept of equal opportunities. The considerations which arise here play an important part in recruitment and selection policies, as discussed in Chapter 8.

# 7

# Human Resource Development

In the NHSE *Priorities and Planning Guidance for the NHS: 1995/6* (EL(94)55) Priority I includes the following:
Arrangements for education and training are improved and produce greater value for money. The agreed changes to Higher Specialist Training (the Calman Report) should be implemented, targets for reduction in junior doctors hours met and there should be full and effective participation in new arrangements for commissioning education and training.

The reference to junior doctors' hours indicates the link between HR planning and development. This link is crucial, and particularly so in the NHS. Clinical and medical staff are expected to have specific qualifications associated with identified bodies of knowledge and courses of training. For example, all doctors employed are expected to have basic medical qualifications from a recognised university within the UK or abroad, approved by the General Medical Council. The institutions concerned have to ensure an adequate supply of such qualified people, and this is true of the other clinical and medical specialties required by the NHS.

The Department of Health lists almost 60 specialty, or branches of medicine, each with sub-specialties. These have to be catered for by the output of medical schools and training programmes at the place of work. Trusts also employ nurses, midwives, physiotherapists, occupational therapists, pharmacists, biomedical scientists, radiographers, dietitians, finance officers, personnel officers, estates officers, chefs, catering staff, laundry staff, portering staff, transport staff, business managers, medical and other secretaries, general managers, supervisors and so on.

All these staff have to be recruited according to predetermined criteria, trained and developed.

The purpose of this chapter is to examine issues associated with overall staff development within the context of a NHS trust.

## General Issues

Virtually the whole of the literature in the general field of training and development expresses concern at the weakness of provision in the UK. Criticism is directed at the whole of our education system and at the practices of employers. We are seen to be failing in comparison with our competitors, whether they be European or Pacific-based. The elitist nature of our general education system and its downgrading of business and commerce is regularly invoked as an explanation for our economic decline since the last quarter of the nineteenth century.

The critique is relatively easy to elaborate – so easy that it leads to such questions being asked as the following: 'But why do British employers fail to train and develop their staff, when ample evidence exists that to do so offers them clear benefits?' (Hyman, in Towers, 1992). A simple answer seems to be that they are so uneducated and badly trained that they either fail to recognise this or are unable to perceive of a solution if they do (for the same reason) or both. The question can, of course, be further extended to UK governments which have been seen to maintain the disjunction between general primary, secondary and higher education and vocational preparation. Ewart Keep, in Sisson (1994), discusses these questions and examines recent attempts in the UK to link the outputs of the educational system to the requirements of industry. He concludes on the following note:

> An editorial in the *Financial Times* (9 May 1990) commented that 'the history of British vocational training is largely a history of failure'. Whether the 1990s will mark a decisive break with this tradition remains to be seen. Given the deep-seated nature of the attitudes and employment structures that have created the problem, it is perfectly possible that Britain will find itself entering the first decade of a new century still lacking an adequate and comprehensive system of education and training for the young.

It could be argued that 'the deep-seated nature of the attitudes and employment structure' in the UK have served its establishment and governments well. The arguments for reform of education and training have been reiterated *ad nauseam* for decades. If the answers were as straightforwardly universally beneficial as proposed, they most certainly would have been taken up. To fall back on attitudes and structure, however deep-rooted, as explanations for attitudes and structure is to resort to tautology.

The NHS has been affected by this general debate, and Keep is as good a source as any for identifying its main ingredients. This debate can be used to rationalise changes which go beyond the need for improved education and training. It can be used to identify the need for 'better' general management, for example. This has been identified as a need in the NHS and has been used as a lever for 'reform' of structures. To the extent that the general debate impinges on the NHS and our trust, it will be referred to. For elaboration of it in more detail, see Keep (Sisson, 1994).

In terms of the above debate, the NHS emerges somewhat differently. Historically it has a high reputation for efficiency. British medical training and practice have excellent worldwide standing and the same is true of its research. Nevertheless it is possible to criticise. The professions contain elements of inflexibility; financial management could be improved; and the same is true of general management. General reforms of training are in place. Some of these are related to the needs of the internal market. A key point is that we do not confuse the needs of this market with the overall issues of training and development. Many of the proposed reforms to training could be seen to be linked to the political objective of increased privatisation of health care provision. This is particularly the case in general management and finance.

**Nurses and Midwives**

Nursing and midwifery staff make up over half of the NHS labour force. There are approximately 500 000 of them, which includes 100 000 not registered, and not training for a registrable qualification. Ninety per cent of this group are female. Project 2000 (UKCC, 1986), introduced changes to nurse and midwifery education. They are now trained in colleges of higher education along with other students, and receive bursaries. They spend 18 months on a general foundation course, followed by 18 months in a specific branch of nursing. Three years is the minimum period required for training to secure registration. The UKCC has proposed that registered nurses (RNs) must undertake a minimum of five days' professional training every three years as a prerequisite for reregistration every three years. Registered midwives (RMs) have been required to undertake refresher courses every five years.

The unregistered nurses referred to above are HCAs, auxiliaries and assistants. NVQs have been accredited for this group of staff. Notionally they can progress to fully qualified professional grades through the NVQ hierarchy. Continued practice for registered nurses requires that they undertake additional formal training every three years. This is obviously essential to ensure proper practice, but imposes additional costs on the employers of such labour. The 1990 NHS Reform and Community Care Act has made GPs more dependent on what are called 'practice nurses', now the fastest growing group of nurses, and the UKCC is examining training requirements.

## Medical Staff

Training for doctors in the UK is undertaken by medical schools which are based in universities. These schools have 'associated' hospitals which provide clinical facilities and patients to help ensure that proper training is undertaken. This requires a well structured relationship between such hospitals and the schools. Before registration with the General Medical Council (GMC) can take place, prospective doctors must spend one year in a hospital as a 'house officer', and hospitals must provide an agreed number of places for these.

Health Authorities are required to provide for postgraduate medical education, and this is done in close liaison with medical schools. They are similarly expected to ensure a provision of management training for medical staff. The basic career structure for doctors is that they qualify from medical school, spend one year in a hospital divided between medical and surgical specialities and then register with the GMC. Following this, they spend, on average, four years as a senior house officer (SHO), working six months in the various specialties before deciding which area of medicine to specialise in.

They could then spend a number of years progressing in their chosen specialty as a registrar or towards becoming a GP. Following this they would then spend two to three years as a senior registrar before becoming eligible for appointment to the position of consultant. Therefore a training period of perhaps 15 years has not been unusual for hospital consultants. This is the system in operation at the time of writing. The Calman Report (1993) has proposed that the training period be reduced to seven to eight years. Doctors would enter their chosen specialty earlier with the registrar and senior registrar periods being consolidated into one 'higher specialist training' period. This change will bring the UK into line with other European countries. It will also increase the supply of consultants.

There are other medical posts, but the above indicates the mainstream and obviously implies important and complex training and development provision.

## Management

Even before the 1990 Act radical changes had taken place in the management structure of the NHS. Reforms consequential to the Griffiths Report (1983) replaced what had become known as 'consensus management'. Under this system, activities were managed by specialists from the relevant disciplines, for example medical, general practice and nursing, who met as a district management team. Nobody in the team had overall leadership or authority and decisions were expected to be achieved by consensus. The Griffiths Report recommended that this be replaced by what has come to be called 'general management', with units of operation having a general manager, or chief executive, with overall control and responsibility. Certain functions – estates, facilities, finance and so on – were devolved from districts to units, and a line management structure began to evolve.

The establishment of the internal market generated other devolved responsibilities, and the need for new management specialties such as financial control, human resource management, quality control, marketing and business management. With distinct purchasers, contracts had to be planned and managed, and ultimately there developed the need for clear strategic planning within a system of control and responsibility. Functional specialists – medical staff and clinicians – have been allocated managerial responsibilities (see Chapter 1). Within this changed context, management training and development needs have been transformed. Managers from other sectors of industry have entered the NHS. The NHS now draws on a much wider range of providers of management training and trained managers. Trusts have to ensure adequate training and development of staff across all these activities and are free to initiate these themselves.

The above represent key groupings of staff within the NHS with highly complex and often highly specialised training and development needs. All other staff have training and development needs. These include paramedical staff, often qualified to degree level, and such groups as porters, clerical, domestic and catering staff. A purpose of this chapter is to examine the structure of provision of such needs within our trust.

**Training and Development: Our Trust**

Training and development are, of course, a part of human resource planning. They have to be linked clearly to the trust business plan and strategy and, as indicated above for clinical and medical staff, meet statutory and professional body requirements. Their planning has to meet the needs of the business plan and reflect projected changes. They have to take account, also, of individual needs and expectations. Notionally every individual in the trust would have a personal development plan. Ideally such plans would be based on appraisal systems. These systems are designed to identify training needs and career development plans, also related to training.

The objective of training and development is to improve both overall and individual performance. Jobs performed by individuals should be linked to the needs of the organisation; these should be examined and relevant job requirements, linked to job descriptions, established, along with acceptable standards of performance. Once this is done, the skills required for acceptable performance of jobs can be linked to the known skills of the labour force.

A variety of methods for doing these things is available. Line managers and employees will provide information on all these matters. The role of the human resource professional is to co-ordinate all the information and fit it to the business plan. Once training and development needs have been identified, they have to be met. This implies an overall plan, the identification of providers to meet these needs, costings and budget allocations. Budget holders have to be identified. Costings and budget allocations for training and development need to be related to some notion of the returns to be secured from them. This requires constant evaluation and analysis. A current trend is to devolve some of the cost to employees.

*Philosophy*

In line with the above, our trust expresses a 'training and development philosophy' in a document produced by the HRM Department. It begins by telling us:

> Training and development should:
>
> 1. Be linked to organisational objectives
> 2. Be responsive to customer needs
> 3. Add value to the organisation
> 4. Be accessible to all staff
> 5. Have top management commitment

The strategy document, more broadly titled 'A Strategy for Education, Training and Development', tells us that the overall aim is to meet 'corporate objectives and sustain business viability.' It also tells us:

> Various senior personnel throughout the organisation will have specific responsibility for ensuring that the many aspects of this strategy are appropriately implemented. The Director of Personnel will have overall responsibility for ensuring that it meets the needs of the organisation, and that it is monitored and reviewed on a regular basis.

The strategy is seen to have three main components under the heading of Organisational Needs. The first of these is described as 'manpower-related', and is defined as 'basic professional and occupational qualifications which clinical staff are required to have in order to provide clinical care. Obligatory professional updating is also included within this category.' It then lays down these requirements for clinical staff, medical staff, professions allied to medicine, finance officers, human resource specialists, estates officers, chefs, business managers, information officers, secretarial staff, chefs, catering assistants, housekeepers, portering and transport staff, and linen room staff. The main components of the strategy are summarised as follows:

**ORGANISATIONAL NEEDS**

_____MANPOWER-RELATED

    – basic professional/occupational
    – updating

_____MAJOR ORGANISATIONAL CHANGES

    – information management and technology
    – trust status
    – new hospital
    – resource management
    – clinicians
    – King's Fund accreditation
    – collaborative care planning
    – clinical directorates
    – clinical support services

_____CORPORATE EFFECTIVENESS

    – management development
    – communications
    – customer care
    – market effectiveness
    – individual competencies
    – team effectiveness
    – public relations

The above summary encapsulates a number of the issues outlined above. All categories of staff are identified, along with basic train-

ing and education requirements for different posts; major organisational changes are identified which will need specific inputs:
general needs are also identified in terms of improving corporate
effectiveness. All human resource staff are identified, for example, as being expected to hold, or be studying for, the Institute of
Personnel and Development (IPD) qualification, while senior
staff are expected to have full IPD membership, with graduate
and/or postgraduate qualification at director level. Staff in posts
which do not require entry qualifications will begin training at
NVQ level 2.

On organisational change requiring planning of training and
development, one item which was identified was information
management and technology, and in particular the installation of
new corporate systems. An information technology centre was
planned which would contain networked computers designed to
support up to ten trainees at a time. Of particular importance was
the development of the clinical information system (CIS)
designed to support medical and clinical needs and the financial
information requirements of the internal market. Specific training plans were established for medical staff, ward sisters and
charge nurses, medical records staff, medical secretaries and the
staff of departments such as X-ray, theatres and pathology. To
support this, there had to be research into the current information use in the hospital, addressing such issues as:

1. clinical diagnosis and procedure definition and how it is collected and reported;
2. managerial use of information for strategic and operational
   purposes, including option appraisal, business planning,
   workload monitoring and improving efficiency in resource
   use;
3. as information becomes available, to explore causal links
   between different data sets;
4. the auditing of services including medical and clinical audit
   to assure standards and promote improvement in the quality
   of services.

This, in itself, represented a formidable training programme.
Open access to training for basic computer skills was also
planned. These plans had to be developed within a programme

of change of the management of information which affected vested interests, creating both human and industrial relations problems. The human resource director had responsibility for ensuring acceptance of systems and the integration of training.

King's Fund accreditation, just another of the development items listed, required all departments to undergo the equivalent of the BS5750 process. An independent, systematic and comprehensive review of procedures and standards was involved. A facilitator had to be specially trained to organise a steering group and project team.

*Management Development*

It is not possible to detail the plans for all groups. Management development is selected as an area of some interest and one generally given some separate treatment in the literature of HRM. Five distinct components of management development were identified:

1.   structured courses leading to a management qualification,
2.   skills-based training,
3.   mentoring,
4.   experiential learning,
5.   professional liaison and networking.

Day-to-day administration of this programme is delegated to a training and development adviser, with the responsibility of ensuring that training begins on appointment, and that first line managers with potential are identified for further training and development. Those selected would, in their second or third year of appointment, be expected to undertake a Certificate in Managing Health Services, run by the trust in collaboration with a local university. Following this are middle management opportunities for university diploma courses, courses run by the Institute of Health Service Management (IHSM) and other relevant courses. Managers aspiring to director level posts would be given opportunities to study for masters degrees. All of this is supported by in-house training on specific matters such as recruitment and selection, equal opportunities, grievance and discipline handling, and such things as managing performance, meetings, finance and attendance.

Programmes of management education were supported by a mentoring system. Mentors were expected to be role models, to act as facilitators and as tutors. This required a programme of mentor selection and training. Experiential learning involves such things as the setting of project work. This would relate to in-house requirements and be supervised. 'Shadowing' of managers was also included. Here, the individual would be attached to a manager as a silent observer of how that manager spent time, established priorities and dealt with other people. Secondment and 'job-swap' arrangements supplemented this. These could be organised by twinning arrangements with other institutions.

A programme of development based on competencies was also established. This is linked to the notion that at every level of job classification there are critical skills required for the adequate performance of such jobs. Previous experience in posts could be used as a demonstration of the acquisition of such competencies. Staff were encouraged to develop portfolios of experience which could give hard evidence of such acquisition. These portfolios could then be submitted to trained assessors, possibly resulting in awards of NVQs between levels 3 and 5.

## The Methods and the Providers

Both the methods and the providers are implied in the above. These would also apply to the elaborate system of training and course provision for all job categories, too numerous to illustrate in this text. Traditional and academic techniques of seminar, lecture and essay writing are combined with mentoring, shadowing, project work, job rotation and exchange, on-the-job training, and distance learning as methods of delivery. Virtually every kind of in-house and external provider is used. External provision is clearly based on carefully developed links with competent and sympathetic institutions. This allows for a degree of cross-fertilisation which can only be sustained as long as such relationships are continuously explored and not allowed to become too comfortable. The National Health Service Training Agency provides an industry-wide researcher into methodologies, course identification and provision, and advice which helps to ensure coherence and effectiveness.

*Appraisal*

This chapter has not explored techniques of appraisal in respect of individual performance and needs. In the context of development the objectives of such techniques are to evaluate performance and potential. There is a variety of such techniques, ranging from rating scales on such things as quality of output, customer responses and so on, to quantitative measures, such as number of FCEs. Objectives may be set and performance assessed according to their level of achievement. Objectives cannot be exhaustively set, and can often be achieved at the expense of those not set. All methods have defects, and none can be a substitute for good management, based on clear supervision and observation, and a capacity for objectivity.

There is no clear evidence from research about how problems of appraisal can be neatly resolved. Managers soon become aware that those managed need systems which they have some confidence in. Medical and clinical appraisal systems are locked into traditional, almost academic systems of qualifications achievements, research outputs and peer review. Leadership qualities play a part, but, certainly in medical assessment, peer review is fairly decisive, although within the professions there are notions of favouritism and establishment style structures. Nevertheless these areas tend to be less contentious than general management areas.

In our trust, a great deal, in other areas, derives from review by supervisors supplemented by HRM advice. Assessment centres are often used for senior levels of management. These make use of outside agencies connected with the health service – the regional office, for example. Here a combination of psychometric testing, team and individual problem solving, with all their defects, might be used in a residential environment.

Probably, as with all organisations, many people can clearly be identified as good managers or as having good potential. Appraisal can be used to rationalise selection for development. It can also be used to attempt to resolve marginal difficulties. Mistakes will be made. Leadership presumably means overseeing a structure which survives and expands. One presumes that checks and balances should be such as to ensure that potential disasters linked to staff performance are soon identified and prevented. Appraisal is probably best seen in these terms rather than as some form of fine-tuning.

*The Economics of Training and Development*

It was noted at the beginning of this chapter that training and development need to be seen as cost-effective: that value added from it exceeds its costs. This is a difficult equation to resolve. Comparative analysis seems to be based on evaluating the proportion of income that so-called 'successful' institutions, or countries, contribute to training compared with less successful (see Hyman, 1992).

Our trust set itself a target of 1 per cent of its income as a training budget. At the time of writing, the sum explicitly allocated was closer to 0.01 per cent. This kind of calculation is extremely problematic. How is the use of in-house resources calculated? What is the cost of on-the-job training? Do low wages for HCAs subsidise training? What proportion of the cost is borne by individuals? If this latter is more in some organisations than in others, is this a sign of valuable commitment and motivation or is it a sign of neglect? What about the 'top-slicing' of NHS budgets for clinical and medical training, whereby sums of money are allocated both nationally and regionally for training?

The cost of training and development looks, superficially, like the easier side of the equation. Questions posed above suggest otherwise. Assessing the value added effect is even more difficult. What can be seen is that there are rewards for successful practice, and in the NHS the advantage of trained professionals in the medical and clinical sphere is obvious, if not specifically quantifiable. Generally the arguments for training and development, when reduced to attempts at quantifiable indicators, become closer to acts of faith than more generalised statements. As one of the authors once heard an academic expert conclude, without any sense of irony, on the subject: 'training and development are difficult to define, most companies do not properly evaluate these, but it is clear that more is needed'.

Specific elements of training can be evaluated. If a person is trained to use a word-processor, specific tests can be applied to assess the results of such training. This is particularly true of skills training. However assessing the ultimate effects of such training on the overall performance of the organisation is more difficult. Training for multi-skilling has been a major development in many UK enterprises. There is little evidence that people make use of this in practice: pressure of work often results in people focusing on their original skills. The more complex training is even more difficult to evaluate in either specific or general terms.

### Conclusion

The argument of this chapter is not that training is neither necessary nor valuable. It was pointed out that the NHS has a history of some success very much related to the quality of medical and clinical training. What is basically being suggested is that the importance of training needs to be contextualised. Training is only one element in performance. There has been a history of employee commitment in the NHS related to the nature of the service. An emphasis on markets, marketing, customers, costs and revenues may generate training needs which equally generate an instrumental relationship to work, with detrimental effects.

In the NHS there are important statutory requirements linked to clinical and medical training. These have proved their effectiveness historically and provide patients with essential protections. New emphases on flexibility could have dangerous consequences; there are very difficult balances to be struck. Emphasis on organisational development and change as objectives of training needs to be carefully considered. As suggested in Chapter 2, the prescriptive nature of many current practices could be shortsighted.

The NHS, like other organisations, has been affected by the emphasis on training initiatives as a necessary component of improving UK industrial efficiency. There is a need for careful 'hands on' management of training and development which cannot be avoided by simply responding to fads and hoping for the best. As suggested in the introduction to this chapter, training is only one and, controversially, an over-rated factor in explaining UK economic performance.

# 8

# Recruitment and Selection

Recruitment is related to human resource planning. The overall objective is to secure a suitably qualified pool of applicants to fit the organisation's requirements. This has to be done in line with legal obligations in respect of such things as equal opportunities and positive discrimination requirements, for example vis-à-vis disabled persons. Many of these were discussed in Chapter 6. It was also seen there that there are objectives to be achieved in line with NHSE guidelines as far as trusts are concerned.

It was also recognised, in Chapter 1, that the supply of potential applicants for particular posts was both external and internal. For many medical posts the external market would be international, for clinical posts predominantly national, whilst for other posts the market would be local. Again, what we see with the NHS is a very complicated structure in terms of its recruitment markets. This has been made more complex by the loss of legal employment rights, in terms of continuity of employment, when moving within the NHS, as a result of the introduction of the internal market.

In general terms line managers are expected to prepare job descriptions and person specifications in respect of jobs to be filled. The human resource department is expected to develop recruitment activities and methodologies in response to information from line managers. This department is also expected to oversee and ensure proper compliance with statutory and NHSE requirements and trust policy. Later we will look at how this is all formally integrated at the level of our trust. First we need to examine certain issues.

## Methodology

The idea that some kind of coherent methodology should be developed for recruitment and selection goes well beyond equal opportunity constraints and the need to ensure that such constraints are observed. This is often summarised in the idea of 'the right person for the right job'. How is it ensured that people are placed in the organisation in such a way that output and performance levels are optimised? Optimisation implies both cost and benefit considerations. Costs relate to pay and other overheads, including the costs of selection, recruitment and placements themselves. Whatever methodologies are used, including those relating to evaluation, ultimate fine-tuning will be a matter of managerial judgement.

Cook (1988:12) refers to the 'classic trio', (application form, reference and interview) which he describes in the following way: 'The *advertisement* attracts *applicants,* who complete and return an *application form.* Some applicants' *references* are taken up; the rest are excluded from further consideration. Candidates with satisfactory references are *short-listed,* and invited for *interview,* after which the post is filled.' It would be possible to turn this into a 'classic quartet', if we add 'induction' and possibly 'probation'. Rejection could follow probation. This 'quartet' then provides a framework for the development of an overall methodology. Although recruitment is generally associated with attracting applicants, and selection with choosing from amongst those applicants, the following account of the 'quartet', which includes induction and probation, and combines the two.

### Advertising

An attempt will be made, by those responsible, to identify the correct advertising outlets, which could include location of advertising in such a way that it contributes to achieving equal opportunities objectives: some publications are more likely to be read by identifiable minorities. Advertisements will also be placed in an attempt to attract optimum responses from appropriately qualified persons. Nursing journals will tend to be read by nurses, medical journals by medically qualified people.

Advertising content can be refined to try to ensure that it is not misleading, and that it minimises the response from unsuitable applicants. 'Word of mouth' might be a supplementary process. Such advertising might be handed over to specialists or recruitment agencies. Senior posts might involve the use of 'headhunters'. In other words, employers will approach the advertising stage from various directions, and this will be related to their continuing evaluation of its effectiveness.

### The Application Form

Application forms can be more or less elaborate, asking for more or less detail. Generally application forms are seeking biographical information, with the belief that such information is relevant to effective selection. Applicants may be asked to submit a curriculum vitae along with the form. This usually gives the applicant the opportunity to select biographical information which he or she believes will be impressive and relevant. Most of the information will be capable of independent verification.

Conclusions are drawn from biographical data. Criminal convictions might automatically exclude applicants, for example. Where organisations create profiles of successful performers based on correlating biographical characteristics with such performance, the methodology may be referred to as 'biodata'. For example, it might be that doctors seen to be successful tend to have a parent who was also a doctor. There may be clusters of biographical data which correlate with 'success': effective workers on a car assembly line might be male, age 26 to 30 years, married with two children and a mortgage. This method of linking biographical data to internal performance-based data is growing in the UK (see Storey and Sisson, 1993).

### Interviews

Interviews are widely used and widely criticised, mainly on the grounds that they are inadequately conducted. There is plenty of advice available on how to model and improve them: see Cook (1988, ch. 4) for example. It is rare that interviewing is used alone – interviews are usually supplemented by application forms and references. Increasingly, references are not used until after the interview.

Interviews might be extended by what is often referred to as 'trial by buffet': invite interviewees the evening before and give them the opportunity to mix with potential colleagues. Colleagues might be consulted for their views. In universities, applicants for academic posts are often asked to make 'presentations', open to academic staff, in sessions prior to the interview programme. The concept of the interview can be extended in a variety of ways. There is no reason why trial by buffet should not be extended to trial by team or group exercise, accompanied by psychological tests of intelligence, ability or personality. Reference was made in the previous chapter to the use of assessment centres in relation to staff development and training. Ultimately people expect to be seen by potential employers, and employers expect to see potential employees. Where exactly the interview fits into the battery of techniques referred to is difficult to assess. There is also the problem of what constitutes 'proper' or 'scientific' use of each of these techniques, and the adequacy of research into them.

A chapter of this type does not allow for detailed examination of the techniques referred to. Cook (1988) gives an excellent overview of the recruitment and selection process and associated research. What can be said is that there seems to be an increased use of biodata, psychometric testing, assessment centres and so on. Where these are used on greenfield sites to select manual workers, who all turn out to have the basic characteristics of the 'mythical' car worker referred to above, it might be that they at least feel that they are part of some elite, which has overcome numerous trials and obstacles. This could have a short-term effect on loyalty and commitment – those selected feel 'special'. A plentiful supply of labour offers the opportunity to experiment and to minimise the possibility of managerial responsibility being questioned. Responsibility can be handed over to the methodology.

Regardless of the issues involved, selecting employees who turn out to be incompetent – or leave soon after appointment – is expensive. Managers need to make intelligent use of what is available and ultimately be prepared to make judgements for which they do accept responsibility.

*Induction and Probation*

Having gambled on an appointment, the likelihood of creating and retaining an effective and motivated employee could be linked to an induction programme. In the USA this is often referred to as an 'orientation programme' or 'indoctrination programme'. According to Torrington and Hall (1991:414), 'New employees are most likely to leave the organisation in the early weeks of employment.' This will obviously vary, depending on the type and level of job, and possibly with the employment situation.

Induction could be seen as part of a process of retention, but it is inextricably bound up with recruitment, especially if what Torrington and Hall say above is true. The process is usually a very basic one involving an introduction to the place of employment, its facilities, introductions to colleagues and so on. Again this could be seen as part of the training programme and its structure and effectiveness will help to produce a competent employee. Probationary or trial periods may be introduced in an attempt to protect the employer against poor selection decisions. These will vary in length depending upon the nature of the work. They will obviously be of significance in terms of the drafting of contracts and the agreement of employee rights during the period of probation. It would also be expected that supervisors would have clear responsibilities in overseeing periods of probation.

Having made these relatively brief comments in respect of general issues relating to recruitment and selection, the next stage is to examine what happens at the level of our trust.

## Recruitment

The trust has devised its own recruitment manual 'to provide practical guidance to managers on 'best practice' in the recruitment and selection of staff and to ensure consistency in approach amongst all managers'.

*Equal Opportunities*

Part 1 of the manual deals with equal opportunities in the process of recruitment and selection. It points out that selection is about discriminating, but that it must be 'fair discrimination'. Managers are referred to the legal problems and to the trust's own equal opportunities policy, and associated policies. Their attention is drawn to the distinction between direct discrimination and indirect discrimination. Direct discrimination takes place when people are treated differently on specific grounds such as race, sex or marital status. The manual tells us:

> Studies both nationally and within the NHS show that direct discrimination remains widespread. Its actual incidence is hard to gauge, as most acts of direct discrimination occur covertly, frequently without the victim's knowledge. This is particularly true in the pre-selection stage of recruitment and it is therefore essential that senior managers ensure that selection practices are subject to scutiny on a regular basis.

Indirect discrimination is seen to occur when a job requirement is applied equally to all but in such a way that a considerable proportion of a particular group might be excluded from applying. A requirement to be able to lift heavy weights might exclude many women and could be shown to be unfair discrimination if the employer could not prove that this requirement was essential to proper performance of the job. Managers are told of the need to recognise that advertisements ought not to be placed in such a way that access to them does not exclude particular groups.

In order to achieve the various targets outlined in Chapter 6, managers are also exhorted to ensure some positive discrimination by:

> recruiting drives to involve job centres, schools, colleges, careers' offices or local community groups located in areas where under-represented groups are concentrated

> indicating in advertisements facilities for job sharing and flexible working arrangements.

To assist in fair selection and achieving equal opportunities objectives, applicants for posts are expected to complete an 'equal opportunities monitoring form'. This asks questions relating to age, gender, marital status, nationality and disability. Marital status is divided into single, married, widowed, divorced and judicially separated. Ethnic origin, alternatively titled racial origin, is divided into white UK, white (other European), Asian, African, Caribbean, other (non-white) and unspecified. Disabled is classified as registered or disabled but not registered. Managers are also expected to debrief unsuccesful candidates for interviews.

*Establishing a Vacancy*

According to the manual it does not follow that, if a person leaves a post, for whatever reason, a vacancy arises. Similarly, if it does create a vacancy, it might be for a post different from that held by the departing employee. Where a person does leave the immediate response should be a *job analysis*. Job analysis is described as the 'the process of examining a job to determine its role and objectives, duties and responsibilities, and the circumstances within which these are achieved or carried out'.

The line manager is allocated the duty of conducting the analysis in conjunction with the departing postholder, colleagues of this person and any immediate supervisor. It is observed that the personnel team will give assistance if required. In order to analyse the job it is stated that the following information be collected: job title; grade; hours of work; to whom responsible; staff managed or supervised; job summary; main duties and responsibilities. Managers are reminded that it is the job which is being analysed, and its requirements, not those duties performed by the previous postholder. A job description, following the analysis, is then expected to be prepared. This is seen as a key management tool, and one which managers should be capable of linking to the business plan. Job applicants will use the job description as a basis for determining their eligibility to apply and suitability for the post.

The next stage in the process is to draw up what is called a *person specification*. This specification turns the job description into a set of characteristics needed by a person capable of performing the job. According to the trust manual, this should contain as a minimum such things as 'qualifications; experience; practical and intellectual skills; special knowledge; disposition/adjustment/attitude'. The contents should be 'job related; expressed in terms which realistically describe abilities; clearly defined; measurable; justifiable; consistently applied to all candidates; weighted in terms of importance'.

All of this is seen as part of the process of proper selection, matching the person to the job and helping to avoid discrimination. The next stage is to seek *vacancy approval*. A vacancy approval form has to be submitted to the chief executive and the director of personnel. Details of the post have to be itemised, including grade and salary, and advertisement information, and a statement of reasons supporting the application has to be included.

### Advertising

It is expected that a vacancy approval be accompanied by a draft advertisement. A 'good advertisement' is expected to attract responses from suitable applicants while deterring unsuitable ones, and create a favourable impression of the trust. It is expected to give a clear job title, as a heading, contain 'selling points' – flexible hours, training opportunities – and contain essential requirements, such as qualifications. It must also state the closing date. Advertisements should contain the trust logo and conclude with the following statements:

'The Trust is an Equal Opportunities Employer'

'The Trust enjoys a Smoke Free Environment'

Locations for advertisements are identified as internally, local job centres, local press, national press, professional journals, recruitment agencies and recruitment fairs. To help in the design of such adverts, the manual gives examples and costings from earlier placements.

### Shortlisting

For all posts a person is designated chairperson of the interviewing panel. On the day following the closing date, the recruitment officer is expected to forward all applications to the chairperson; the shortlisting process is expected to be completed within one working week, and the shortlist returned to the recruitment officer. The recruitment officer is then expected to invite candidates to interview within two working days, giving ten working days' notice to them. Candidates who have not been shortlisted are expected to be notified within the two working days.

The first stage of shortlisting should be to discard applications from those without appropriate qualifications or experience. It is suggested that the next stage might be based on a threefold classification of applicants into suitable, marginal and unsuitable. These decisions must be closely related to the person specification. Whether or not marginal cases will be shortlisted depends upon the number of applicants and posts to be filled. Once the shortlist is compiled, a shortlisting and interview record form must be completed and this must give explanations of why candidates were not shortlisted.

On receipt of the shortlist, the recruitment officer invites candidates to interview, giving details of date, time, venue, panel members, any presentations that might be expected and medical clearance requirements.

## References

References are requested by the recruitment officer from the named referees of the shortlisted candidates. Candidates are expected to name a minimum of two referees (three for medical posts). According to the manual, references 'are obtained to validate character, performance and attitude in the previous work environment'. It is suggested, therefore, that they should try to seek information which can be objectively assessed – attendance records, length of service and so on. Obviously, with more senior posts, referees might be expected to offer opinions on suitability and competence for the particular post. Referees will be sent full job descriptions and stamped addressed envelopes.

The reference process might be made complicated, depending upon the policy of the employer. In our trust, a reference is only sought for shortlisted applicants, and consulted after the interview has taken place. Other employers might use the reference as part of the shortlisting process. Applications might appear suitable, but be discarded after references have been read and thus not included on the shortlist. Occasionally applicants request that references are not taken up unless they are shortlisted, possibly because they do not wish to influence the attitude of their current employer, who may see them as disloyal, or as 'on the way out' and therefore not suitable for promotion. Being invited to interview puts the applicant in a stronger position vis-à-vis their own employer, sometimes, because this suggests that in order to retain an employee inducements may need to be offered. Oral references might be obtained by telephone, and this might generate greater frankness.

Using references after an interview is based on the notion that they are not always reliable, and that the panel might be unduly influenced by them. Interviewing 'cold' might produce a more objective assessment. The reference can then be used to identify anything outstanding which might disqualify the person chosen. The difficulty here is that avoidable costs might have been incurred.

### Occupational Health Screening

The occupational health department is expected to screen short-listed candidates on health grounds. It therefore receives lists of shortlisted candidates and job descriptions. A form is sent from this department to these candidates, to be completed and returned before the interviews. The purpose is to relate medical condition to job requirements. It may also help to select health promotion initiatives in respect of groups of employees once in post; these could be as basic as immunisation or vaccination programmes.

### Interview

The manual makes some basic textbook points about interviewing skills. Generally, as indicated above, the guidelines are devised for mainstream staff rather than senior managers or medical staff. This is reflected in the advice that a good selection interview should last a 'minimum of 15 minutes' and that a panel would consist of a minimum of two people. Nevertheless much of the advice would apply across the whole job spectrum.

There are plenty of texts which give advice on interviewing techniques. Here we are only concerned to note that in our trust interviews play a key part in the selection process. Panel members in trust interviews are advised to rate each candidate against each job requirement on a numerical scale of discrete numbers from 0 to 3. This allows total scores to be awarded as a basis for making the final decision. The panel is expected to make a decision immediately after the interview and to notify candidates of the decision on the day. Written confirmation is to be forwarded within five days of the interview.

The above is an account of the appointment procedure for non-medical staff below the level of senior managers. Senior management and medical staff are subjected to different procedures.

## Senior Managers

These are essentially managers with directorial responsibilities. The major difference here is that such posts involve the equivalent to an assessment centre approach. Outside, specialist consultants are used to implement and validate psychometric testing assessments and observation of group tasks. The group tasks involve the shortlisted candidates. There will be a series of one-to-one interviews with relevant executives. This is followed by a panel interview which involves board members and external assessors. Each panel interview is preceded by a short presentation to the panel by the candidate on a selected topic relevant to the job.

This process takes two days. It also involves a dinner on the first evening. The panel will take into account information from all of the encounters referred to. Applications and shortlisting are mediated through the specialist consultancy agency responsible for organising the assessment centre processes.

Applicants for such posts are provided with detailed and elaborate job descriptions. They will have explained to them trust objectives in general and those specifically relevant to the post. Curriculum vitae are expected to provide extensive biodata and to address the trust objectives in terms which illustrate the special qualities which the applicant can bring to bear on these. The curriculum vitae is of considerable importance in the shortlisting process. Potential applicants are also invited to contact and meet the chief executive to discuss the post in detail before submitting an application.

**Medical Staff**

The most senior appointments are to the position of consultant. Such appointments are governed by statutory instruments. These instruments require an appointments procedure to be followed. For example, where a trust proposes to make an appointment there are legal requirements as to the nature and number of publications in which advertisements should be placed. The instruments also lay down rules about the constitution of what is called the Advisory Appointments Committee (AAC).

The region in which our trust is located provides detailed guidance on the appointments of consultants. This guidance is actually put together by the postgraduate medical and dental education department of the region. It begins by pointing out that the timescale for the establishment of an Advisory Appointments Committee is a *minimum* of three months. A job description and person specification is drawn up by consultants concerned and the chief executive. This has to be approved by the Regional Adviser of the 'appropriate Royal College'.

Once a job description is approved, advertisements can be placed. Statute requires that a minimum of two appropriate journals be used and in this case these are *The British Medical Journal* and *The Lancet*. The next stage is setting up an Advisory Appointments Committee. Such a committee's constitution can be derived from a recommended seating plan, circulated by the region, for the conduct of the interview. An AAC will usually include a 'lay' chairperson; normally the trust chairperson will aim to chair all AACs. There will be a minimum of three medical representatives from the trust. These will include the medical director, the clinical director of the specialty concerned and a consultant from that specialty. There will also be present a Royal College representative, a university representative and the chief executive of the trust. Another 'interested' consultant from the directorate may also attend and on occasions an outside assessor, such as a senior consultant in the specialty, might be invited to advise the panel. A personnel officer will attend to provide administrative assistance and to help ensure that the proper procedure is adhered to. The voting members of the AAC will receive copies of all applications and each member will be invited to submit a shortlist of up to four applicants. From these a final shortlist of applicants, usually four, is constructed.

References are sought for shortlisted applicants and members of the committee receive these. Interviews are arranged, the recommendation being that these take place in alphabetical order of the candidates' surnames. It is the chairperson's duty to ensure that the interview is conducted in accordance with the statutory instruments. There has to be a quorum and, if a vote takes place, there must be a majority in favour. The chairperson has a vote, but no casting vote. It is expected that candidates remain available until interviews have been completed and the successful candidate is called back to the committee to be informed of its decision.

The committee is bound by equal opportunities laws and policies. At the time of writing the procedure for appointing consultants is under review and a new statutory instrument is being prepared. Other medical staff, registrars, senior registrars and so on, are appointed in accordance with similar procedures. Shortlisted applicants for medical posts are subject to occupational health checks. Where an appointee has substantial access to children, a 'disclosure of criminal background' form is enclosed with the application form.

Because of the nature of medical posts it is clear that there has to be statutory guidance on appointments to them. There has to be Royal College approval to guarantee expertise, and appointees have to produce a certificate of the General Medical Council. All of these factors reduce, quite properly, the freedoms of general management, with their views being allowed for at the shortlisting and appointments stages.

## Conclusion

It is a platitude of the literature that bad selection is costly. This is slightly more than a tautology. Appointing people who do not perform well, or who leave, is undoubtedly expensive. Naturally those responsible for employing people will seek ways of ensuring proper selection. This concept is fraught with difficulties, in particular that of selecting some independent variable against which successful or unsuccessful selection can be tested.

One advantage of the statutory registers affecting many NHS staff is that being on the register can be defined as a necessary requirement. This, whatever the qualities of the register's composition, partly simplifies the process of selection. However, this is no guarantee that such a member will meet job performance requirements. There is also the problem of the way what constitutes proper performance requirements is determined. This latter point has long been regarded as something of a conundrum. Nearly 40 years ago, Whyte (1960), referred to what he called a *self confirming profile* – interviewers tend to be seeking people most like themselves. Tests, interviews and so on, are all devised to incorporate the values of those who use and construct them. There may be nothing wrong with this. The problem is that the process simply replicates the structure – if the methods are reliable. This is probably why organisations with problems usually have to use external catalysts to provoke change.

In the NHS, statutory intervention has provoked radical changes in perceptions of what is required from job holders. Financial considerations have grown to compete with medical considerations. Applicants for senior medical positions are expected to have shown some concern for developing their management skills. More are adding Masters of Business Administration (MBAs) to their curriculum vitae. Line managers and board members are being selected more on their capacity to take 'tough' decisions in a cost cutting environment. Whether this is 'right' in some absolute sense is open to debate.

The above illustrates the special factors at play in recruitment and selection in the NHS. Statutory intervention is of some significance in these processes. If patients, clients, customers, or whatever else they may be called, are to be protected it may reasonably be presumed that this form of intervention will continue, probably in a weakened form, however privatised health provision becomes.

# 9

# Redundancy

No current account of the role of HRM in the NHS can omit consideration of the question of redundancy. It has been said that part of the role of the HRM director is to 'switch the lights off on the way out'. A variant is that the HRM director should make him or herself redundant through the process of devolving the functions of HRM to line managers.

Chapter 1 suggested that strategic planning was bedevilled by the uncertainty of the future, and in the NHS by the 'wild cards' of political expediency. Technology changes require a strategy of hospital merger and closure; political considerations require that this is not open to clear communications, but that it should be manipulated as surreptitiously as possible. In the case of our trust, its 1995/6 business plan was deemed to be based on service provision and prices which would lead to a deficit. The size of the deficit was predicted by the RO. How it was calculated, and in fact how subsequent variations on its initial size were also calculated, never became clear. First out was the chief executive, given an afternoon to clear his desk. The deficit was to be resolved by reorganisation of service through what was described as a merger with another trust, but which was in fact a takeover. An acting chief executive was appointed, and our trust board was disbanded. Furthermore, an interim arrangement from 1 April 1995 was made to the effect that our trust would be overseen by the board of the other trust pending full takeover on 1 April 1996. The takeover trust laid down conditions which included immediate action to secure £800000 savings from management and support staff.

All of the above, including initiating statutory and agreed consultation procedures, took place within one week.

## Redundancy: Statutory Provision

The statutory definition of redundancy derives from the Employment Protection (Consolidation) Act of 1978 (EP(C)A) and the Trade Union Reform and Employment Rights Act of 1993 (TURERA). Redundancy is defined in the following way:

> (a) the employer ceases to carry on the business in which the employee was engaged – or closes the place in which s/he was working;
> (b) the business ceases to require people with the particular skills of the employee or needs fewer of them to carry out the work;
> (c) the dismissal is for a reason not related to the individual concerned or for a number of reasons all of which are not so related.

The provision under (c) above was introduced by TURERA 1993. This allows for reorganisations of work to take place which might require fewer workers but do not create redundancies which fall into the definitions in (a) and (b). Where an employee can demonstrate that his or her post has been made redundant then that employee is entitled to certain payments by law.

Statutory payments for redundancy date back to the Redundancy Payments Act of 1965. Apart from this provision for compensation for dismissal arising from specific circumstances, there were no other provisions beyond what the contract required. For example, an employee with one week's notice in his or her contract could be given that notice, or pay in lieu, and the employer did not have to give a reason. The Act of 1965 allowed the employee to claim compensation if the employee could demonstrate redundancy was the actual reason. Industrial tribunals heard such claims. Compensation was based on length of service with the employer. At the time, employment levels were high and there was considerable overstaffing in industry, a part of which was due to employers hoarding scarce labour. The act was designed to encourage labour mobility by reducing labour resistance to redundancy. It also provided rebates to employers to offset the costs incurred by the payments. There was the notion that released employees would quickly move into other jobs where they were more needed (Davies and Freedland, 1993).

The 1971 Industrial Relations Act introduced the concept of unfair dismissal. This required employers to have a reason for dismissal and to act fairly in the manner of the dismissal. Reasons for dismissal had to be fair; under the EP(C)A 1978 these include capability or qualifications; conduct; redundancy; some other statutory enactment or some other substantial reason. Employees could now bring claims to industrial tribunals on the grounds that their dismissal was unfair. Compensation could include payment for lost redundancy entitlements, along with compensation for loss of earnings and other benefits. A considerable body of case law has developed around this concept of unfair dismissal.

Employers are expected to prove a fair reason for dismissal, that that reason was good cause, that agreed procedures – on discipline or redundancy, for example – had been followed, and that the employee had been given full information and opportunity to challenge and appeal against the employer's actions. It follows from the above that there could be such a wrong as unfair redundancy dismissal. Between 1965 and 1971, employers often appeared before industrial tribunals arguing that a redundancy had not taken place in order to avoid paying compensation. Now they often appear arguing that redundancy was the real reason in order to avoid additional payments of compensation for acting unfairly.

The 1971 Act, and growing unemployment, has produced a situation where the emphasis is on some rights to job ownership and security. Redundancy for many is not a way of becoming mobile in the job market but of becoming totally excluded from it. For some it is a tragedy. For the HRM director, the management of redundancy presents onerous duties in respect of the law and the task of dealing face to face with those people affected by it.

*Compensation*

A recent survey (IRS, 1995:5), showed that 90 per cent of the companies responding provided compensation for redundancy in excess of the statutory minimum. This is also true of our trust, operating under Whitley provisions. For statutory redundancy compensation an employee has to have a minimum period of service of two years beyond the age of 18 years. Service prior to the age of 18 years, or beyond normal retirement age, is not taken into account. For service between the ages of 18 or over, but under 22 years, half a week's pay is awarded for each qualifying year of service; from 22 or over, but under 41, one week's pay; and from 41 to 64, one and a half week's pay. There are limits to a week's pay – currently £205 – and to the number of years which can be taken into account – currently 20 years. This produces a maximum statutory payment of £6150. Employers are free to agree and make additional payments.

In the NHS, section 45 of the National Whitley Agreement deals with redundancy. There is no limit to a week's pay. Completion of service between the age of 18 years and 22 years attracts one half a week's pay; from 22 to 41, one week's pay; and from 41 to 64, one and one half. All of this is limited to thirty weeks in total. Employees not entitled to benefits under the NHS superannuation scheme receive two weeks for all years at 18 or over, plus an additional two weeks' pay being made for service beyond the age of 41 years, to a maximum of 16 weeks. This produces an overall maximum of 66 weeks. A week's pay can be calculated as 7/365ths of annual salary at date of termination, or the weekly wage according to Whitley Agreements, whichever is most beneficial.

The above would represent substantial costs to our trust, already notionally in deficit. Redundancy payments are consequently funded by the RO, through the purchasers. This obviously fits the strategic role attributed in this text to ROs.


### Fair Redundancy

As implied above, for a redundancy to comply with the law it must be genuine. Using redundancy as an excuse to replace somebody could lead to an unfair dismissal claim by the replaced person. Employers may attempt to obscure dismissal for some other reason by 'phoney' restructuring.

Where genuine redundancies occur, it may be that only a proportion of identical or similar posts need to be lost. This raises the question of which particular posts, and obviously leads to choices between postholders, rather than posts per se. In other words, some individuals, rather than others, will ultimately be selected for redundancy dismissal. The law requires fair selection, and clearly discrimination on race, sex, trade union membership or non-membership would be unacceptable. In practice, criteria for selection could be indirectly, or less obviously, discriminatory. Selecting part-time rather than full-time workers could discriminate against females. The same may also be true of 'last in first out' (LIFO) as a method of selection. LIFO can be cheap for employers in the short run, but in the long run it can mean, where service-based increments exist, that highly paid employees are being retained.

Generally employers should seek voluntary redundancy as a starting-point, although it might well be that in the interests of the business certain volunteers may be rejected. According to the Employment Appeals Tribunal, in *Williams* v. *Compair Maxam Ltd*, criteria for selection should be chosen which 'as far as possible do not depend solely upon the opinion of the person making the selection, but can be objectively checked against such things as attendance record, efficiency at the job, experience, or length of service'. In the same case it was suggested that, where unions are recognised, there should be consultation and, if possible, agreement on selection criteria. The trend appears to be to use efficiency criteria, and fall back on LIFO as a last resort (IRS, 1995).

The Trade Union and Labour Relations (Consolidation) Act 1992 (TULR(C)A) lays down the notification and consultation requirements for redundancies where a trade union is recognised. The trade union, which could be a shop steward, should be notified in writing of impending redundancies. This notice begins the consultation period, and must begin at the earliest opportunity. If more than 100 employees are to be dismissed within 90 days, then notice must be given at least 90 days before the first dismissal, or, if more than 10 within 30 days, at least 30 days before. The same notice must be given to the Department of Employment. Where less than 10 are involved, the requirement is for as much notice as possible. The trade union and individual employees are entitled to receive the following information:

explanation of why the redundancies are taking place;
the numbers and descriptions of those employees involved;
the selection criteria for redundancy;
how the dismissals will be carried out and over what time period;

if redundancy payments are above the statutory minimum, what these are and how they are calculated.

Employees notified of impending redundancies are entitled to their full period of contractual notice from when they are made redundant. This is, of course, added to their employment period for the calculation of payments.

TURERA 1993 requires employers to consult union representatives with a view to reaching agreement. Consultation should cover all the options: voluntary redundancy, redeployment, selection criteria, natural wastage, time off to seek new employment and so on. An employer may attempt to avoid a dismissal by offering suitable alternative employment. Such an offer must be made within four weeks of the termination of the old contract. Employees have the right to a trial period, and to challenge the offer on the grounds that the new post is substantially different, or involves some substantial material change, such as excessive travel.

Failure to consult a trade union can lead to protective awards to compensate individuals for loss for the period during which the consultation should have taken place. Failure to consult the individual could lead to an unfair dismissal claim. Failure to give adequate time off to seek alternative employment could result in a tribunal claim against the employer. In *Commission* v. *UK* (1994), the European Court of Justice decided that the UK was in breach of EU law by only consulting the representatives of recognised trade unions in redundancy situations. The implication would seem to be that there is a requirement to consult representatives of the workforce, in such situations, even where no trade union is recognised. This has not yet been subject to interpretation, but it does offer interesting possibilities for the future.

The above gives some general background to redundancy issues. What follows is an account of dealing with redundancy in practice at the level of our trust.

*Redundancy at Trust Level*

The first wave of redundancies, set at approximately 40 posts, required a 30-day consultation period. This began on 1 April 1995. A consultation document was prepared outlining the policy to be adopted. The areas where such redundancies could take place, and the number of posts, were identified and asserted by the takeover trust. The document began by identifying the cause of impending redundancies, an estimated £7.8 million deficit leading to a merger. It pointed out that immediate reductions in posts were necessary to secure £800 000 of savings. The timescale was given as follows: posts to be made redundant from 31 July 1995; notice to be given on 1 May 1995. This was followed by inclusion of the statutory definition of redundancy. Posts 'at risk' were described as '40 senior management, middle management, secretarial and clerical support staff'. Maintaining an effective and efficient service was given as the major consideration in choosing posts, and this consideration would be taken into account in respect of volunteers. Volunteers were invited to make their wishes known with a guarantee of privacy.

The document committed the trust to minimising dismissals by examining all proposals in respect of redeployment, job-sharing, part-time working and finding suitable alternative employment. Requests for early retirement were invited; a freeze was placed on recruitment; and the examination of the current use of temporary staff, which could be reduced, was suggested. Selection criteria for compulsory dismissals were related to the needs of the merged trusts. Confidential counselling and career advice were offered. Appeals against redundancy were to be lodged within seven days of notice being given.

The nature of the posts 'at risk' at this time did not attract the involvement of trade unions. Some of the posts identified by the takeover trust were actually vacant. It began to appear that the initial phase would ultimately result in about 20 compulsory redundancies. Nevertheless many of those in posts associated with those immediately 'at risk' realised that there was probably no future in a merged trust and job searches began. Some medical and clinical staff, previously employed by the takeover trust, also began to search for jobs.

The new hospital had developed from something like 30 years of political pressure for the integrated provision of health services to the community concerned. A merged trust would mean that some services would now be located in the takeover trust, in a separate geographical location, approximately ten miles away. This obviously reduced NHS costs, through economies of scale, but could increase the costs borne by patients and visitors as a result of extra travel. The rationale was that the predicted deficit represented an unwillingness on the part of the purchasers, acting as proxies for the 'consumers', to purchase at our trust prices.

Some reaction from the community was expressed. However this had no noticeable effect on RO strategy. At this stage, the unions were offering no organised resistance. It was possible that the next phase of redundancies might have more of an impact.

*Staff Support Systems*

Torrington and Hall (1991:391) tell us: 'The large scale of redundancies in recent years has produced a variety of managerial initiatives to mitigate the effects. One of the most constructive has been a redundancy counselling service.' Our trust produced a folder of documentation to help staff.

The reorganisation of services produced direct redundancies and situations where postholders were invited to compete for some of the remaining posts. Each trust in the takeover had a personnel director, and now only one such post would be needed. This would be opened to competition between the current incumbents, prior to national advertising if neither was successful. Given the new structure, this would actually be seen as a new post.

The folder of documentation for staff was titled 'Staff Support Systems'. It contained three main sections:

1. **Counselling services**   Occupational health provided a confidential counselling service where the problem was personal or job related. The chaplaincy became contactable on a 24-hour telephone service. A local church made available trained volunteers, who also offered counselling. Most of the counselling provided by these agencies was concerned with dealing with stress. Occupational health was used intensively. Stress would be a factor generated by the reorganisation and would affect many people not directly involved in redundancy.

   Counselling specifically related to redundancy was made available by the Central England Enterprise Council (CENTEC). CENTEC notionally charge people for their services if they are in full time employment. Contributions to CENTEC from our trust ensured that its provision was free to individuals. CENTEC linked its counselling to other services, such as help in job search via workshop training.

2. **Workshops to support job search** Workshops were run on a 'drop in' basis at the trust education centre. These included the obvious topics of 'Where to Start Finding Another Job', 'How to Write an Effective Curriculum Vitae', 'Interview Preparation and Procedures'. CENTEC also provided seminars under the title of 'Self Marketing Workshops'. They also made available documentation designed to give confidence, and this included a list of competencies to jog the memory for c.v. purposes. Competencies included such things as flexibility, adaptability, sociability, teamworking, numeracy and so on – all with some explanation. Sample c.v.s were included as guidance on how to complete them. Some explanation of the recruitment and selection methods used by organisations was also included, for example psychometric testing, personality assessment and so on.

3. **Services that can provide additional support and guidance** This section of the folder gave addresses of other organisations – such as recruitment agencies – with some description of the services they provide.

These services attracted a considerable response, and were partly developed as a result of requests made by staff. How effective these are in terms of alleviating the problems of redundancy, from joblessness itself to the associated stresses, remains to be researched.

## Conclusion

The purpose of this chapter has been to identify the main issues associated with redundancy and the role of the human resources department in it. It has also, as a result of circumstances, provided something of a case study. Given the scale of job losses in recent years, the provisions we have discussed offer some alleviation of the situation to people affected but can hardly be linked to the earlier objectives of securing a more mobile labour force. The extent of redundancy does not make it more palatable. This will equally be the case for NHS employees. According to Armstrong (1990:807–8):

> Redundancy, or what is now sometimes called 'downsizing', is the saddest and often the most difficult problem concerning people personnel managers have to deal with. There are five things which can be done to make it less painful:
>
> 1.   Plan ahead to avoid redundancy.
> 2.   Use other methods of reducing numbers or man-hours to avoid or minimise the effects of redundancy.
> 3.   Call for voluntary redundancy.
> 4.   Develop and apply a proper redundancy procedure.
> 5.   Provide help in finding new jobs, ie 'outplacement', as it is now called.

Our trust has attempted all of the above. Part of the theme of this book is that planning ahead is difficult where the future may not only be obscure, but be made deliberately so to minimise political consequences.

# 10

# Case Studies

These case studies are included for two main purposes. The first is to give some insight into the process of dealing with change in the NHS in the mid-1990s. They are directly derived from actual cases and thus have some historical significance. Both are also pointers to the future in terms of potential problems. It is hoped that they will provide a clearer picture of issues discussed in the text. The second purpose is to provide a teaching device. Each case could be used for group work, with groups reporting back on what they consider to be the main issues. Similarly, they can be used for role-play. Students could be divided into management and union teams and be asked to meet to negotiate the issues. As negotiating exercises, they are open-ended: there is no obvious outcome. In real life such scenarios will be resolved in accordance with the power and determination of the parties. As classroom exercises, they could run from a minimum of three hours to several days. Tutors have to be clear about their teaching objectives.

A short version could be used to identify basic issues such as the setting of objectives, the allocation of roles and intra-organisational aspects of bargaining. In some cases, exercises could be simplified by having only one union involved; in other cases the number of unions might be increased, depending upon the objectives of the exercise. For example, unions will have separate agenda. In fact, the exercise may simply focus on unions negotiating with each other in order to achieve a common proposal.

The exercise could concentrate on problems of bargaining structure – reconciling single table bargaining with divergent functional interests. On the other hand, the tutor may wish to focus on the elements of bargaining theory, or teaching negotiating skills. However the case studies are used, the tutor should have a clear framework of analysis. The following represents suggestions.

1.  What are the key roles which emerge within bargaining teams? These should be allowed to develop dynamically, from within the groups, and groups should be interrogated on how these were allocated and what precisely were the groups' expectations about the way these roles should be played. For example, the role of 'lead spokesperson' invariably emerges. What alternatives are available in terms of the exercise of this role?
2.  Did the team set objectives? If so, how did they do this? This should be related to concepts of target positions.
3.  In terms of the agenda for the negotiations, did they include items simply to offer bargaining counters, or did they all represent serious objectives? Either way, what was the strategy in terms of the use of argument and proposition? What is the role of argument in negotiations?
4.  The dynamics of the negotiations could be examined. How were they structured in terms of presentations, 'state of the nation' statements, views of members and so on? What is the purpose of adjournments and what is the mechanism for seeking these?
5.  How is agreement on issues signalled, and how are full agreements drafted?
6.  What is the role of the trust board in negotiations? How are union members involved in the making of claims and in settlements?

All of the above should be analysed in terms of the key literature on bargaining theory (see in particular Walton and McKersie, 1965). For a summary of the approach outlined above, see also Burchill (1992:ch. 9).

**Case Study 1**

This consists of two *draft* recognition agreements. The first is proposed by the staff side and begins with a list of the unions to be recognised, whilst the second is a draft from management. There is no disagreement between the drafts over the unions to be recognised. The only difference is that UNISON appears first in the staff side list, and last in the management list. This is the only difference between the lists as they appear in the two documents. Apart from this, all other unions are listed alphabetically in both drafts. They have been included here in the staff side to illustrate the complexity of NHS union structure, and the consequent intra-organisational bargaining problems.

(STAFF SIDE DRAFT) Recognition Agreement

Healthside NHS Hospital Trust

1  *The Parties*

The Agreement is between Healthside NHS Hospital Trust, 'the Trust', and the following Trade Unions, 'the Unions'.

UNISON (incorporates BAOT)
British Dietetic Association
British Medical Association
British Orthoptic Society
Chartered Society of Physiotherapists
Electrical, Electronic, Telecommunications and Plumbing Union
General, Municipal and Boilermakers Union (*sic*)
Manufacturing, Science and Finance Union (includes Hospital Physicists Association, Guild of Hospital Pharmacists and Health Visitors Association)
Royal College of Midwives
Royal College of Nursing
Society of Radiographers
Union of Construction, Allied Trades and Technicians

2  *Commitment*

The Trust and the Unions are committed to the Trust's Mission Statement and the long-term success of the Trust.

3    *Recognition*

The Trust recognises the Unions listed above and that representation of employees by them is of mutual benefit. These Unions have sole bargaining rights at the Trust on all matters relating to the terms and conditions of employees with the exception of general and senior managers who wish to negotiate their pay individually. The Trust will encourage employees to join the appropriate recognised union, and agrees to provide facilities for collection of subscriptions at source.

4    *Agreed Principles*

Pursuit of common objectives will be achieved via consultation, negotiation and information sharing.

4.1    Consultation

An exchange of views based on the principle that the mere passage of information is not consultation – it must include the opportunity to influence decisions and their application.

4.2    Negotiation

A formal process for the purpose of reaching agreement and avoiding disputes. The scope of such negotiation shall be as defined in Section 29 (1) of TULRA 1974 as amended by Section 6 Par. 178 (i) of TULR(C)A 1992, and any relevant subsequent amendments to legislation.

4.3    Information

The parties are committed to sharing information for bargaining purposes in accordance with ACAS Code of Practice No 2 and Par. 181 of TULR(C)A 1992, and relevant subsequent legislation.

5    *Representation*

5.1    The Trust agrees to recognise accredited representatives, local branch officials and full-time officers of the Unions for all the purposes of this Agreement.

5.2    The Unions will notify the Trust of accredited representatives and their constituencies. Management will only engage in collective bargaining with accredited representatives of the Unions and their full-time officers.

5.3 Accredited representatives will be granted access to necessary facilities to enable them to carry out their duties and to required time off for such purposes and for training. In addition the Trust will grant paid time off to allow accredited representatives to play a role in wider Union activities.

## 6 *Committees*

6.1 Joint Negotiating Committee (JNC)

6.2 This JNC will negotiate terms and conditions of employment for employees covered by collective arrangements across all functions within the Trust.

6.3 Each of the Unions will elect one accredited representative to serve on the JNC, except UNISON which will elect three.

6.4 Union members of the JNC will elect a staff side secretary.

6.5 Full-time officers of the Unions may attend the JNC meetings.

6.6 Expert witnesses may be called by the Unions to aid the JNC.

6.7 Trust representation will include the Chief Executive Officer and the Director of Human Resource Management.

6.8 The Staff Side of the JNC will elect a chairperson for each separate negotiation.

6.9 Failures to agree will be dealt with under the Collective Disputes Procedure.

6.10 If there is a failure to agree at the final stage of the Collective Disputes Procedure it will be referred to ACAS for conciliation/arbitration.

## 7 *Functional Negotiating Committees (FNCs)*

There will be four FNCs dealing with issues specific to them. They will be representative of the following groups:

**FNC ONE**

Nurses, Midwives, Health Visitors, District Nurses, Health Care Assistants/Nursing Assistants.

Unions recognised (one representative each): RCN; UNISON; RCM; MSF.

**FNC TWO**

A&C, ASC, Maintenance, Chaplains.

Unions recognised (one representative each): UNISON; AEEU; UCATT; GMB.

**FNC THREE**

MSLOs, PT'B', Physiotherapists, Occupational Therapists, Speech Therapists, Psychologists, Radiographers, Chiropodists, Pharmacists, Dietitians, Art Therapists.

Unions recognised (one representative each): UNISON; BDA (Dietitians); CSP; MSF; SoR.

**FNC FOUR**

Medical and Dental Staff.

Unions recognised (one representative each): BMA; BDA (Dentists); BOS.

The FNCs will operate in accordance with the procedures outlined for the JNC.

### 8   *Joint Consultative Committee (JCC)*

8.1   Consultation, as defined in 4.1 above, will take place in the JCC. It will examine all Trust business plans, service objectives and policies. Members of the JCC will be given full opportunity to comment on these and to raise any other issues they consider relevant to the fair, efficient and effective running of the Trust.

8.2   Each of the Unions will be entitled to send one member to meetings of the JCC and pre- meetings of these members.

9.2 The JCC will meet on the afternoon of the last Thursday of every calendar month.

Review of this agreement may be sought at each anniversary of it.

Provision is made in the above draft agreement for it to be signed by a full-time officer of each of the listed unions.

(MANAGEMENT SIDE DRAFT) Recognition Agreement

Healthside NHS Hospital Trust

1 Parties to the Agreement
This Agreement is between the Trust and the Unions.

2 Recognition
The Healthside NHS Hospital Trust recognises the Unions listed in the Appendix for the purposes of this Agreement.

3 Mutually Agreed Principles

3.1 The Trust and the Unions have the common objectives of:

a. ensuring the efficient operation of the Trust in the interest of patients, purchasers of services, the Trust, and all employees.

b. the maintenance of excellent management/employee relations and communications.

3.2 Both sides agree that achieving the above objectives shall be by:

a. Negotiation, for the purpose of reaching joint agreements.

b. Consultation, which means providing a genuine opportunity to influence decisions and their application.

c. Communication, which means keeping each side fully informed of relevant matters.

3.3   The Unions recognise and acknowledge management's responsibility to plan, organise and manage the activities of the Trust within available income.

3.4   The Trust believes that fully representative Trade Unions improve employee relations and will encourage employees to belong to an appropriate Trade Union.

## 4   Scope of Recognition

4.1   Those issues which directly relate to employment shall normally be dealt with by negotiation, including the following matters:

a. basic pay, pay structures and Terms and Conditions of Employment for staff on Trust Contracts.

b. employment/personnel policies, procedures and issues arising from their application.

c. the organisation of work and working practices.

4.2   The following matters are excluded from Trust-wide negotiating within the pay negotiating machinery:

market supplements to pay scales, or rates

rates of performance related pay and any payments to individuals, or groups, under such schemes

ad hoc payments, including those for the purpose of transferring any individual, or group of staff, from Whitley to Trust Contracts

the above matters may arise in direct discussions with particular staff groups

4.3   Other matters which will normally be dealt with by consultation include:

the Business Plan of the Trust

the overall financial plan and position of the Trust

any operational decisions which may have staffing implications, including implications for job security

working conditions including health, safety and welfare

5   Representation and Facilities

5.1   The Trust agrees to recognise accredited local representatives and full time officials of the Trade Unions listed.

5.2   The Trust shall provide time-off and other facilities for representatives of recognised Trade Unions.

5.3   The recognised Trade Unions agree to provide the Trust annually with evidence of membership numbers.

5.4   The Trust accepts its obligations to disclose reasonable and relevant information needed for the purpose of collective bargaining. The Trust will operate the provisions of the relevant ACAS Code of Practice.

6   Disputes
Any disputes arising from the joint committees shall be dealt with through the Trust's Disputes Procedure.

**Intra-organisational Bargaining: the Unions**

The above provides the essence of draft proposals made at a trust in early 1995. For exercise purposes students should have access to the ACAS Codes of Practice 2 and 3 and relevant statutes. The draft staff side proposal could be used to examine intra-organisational bargaining issues which arise between unions. For example, there is the political significance of the dominance of UNISON. The RCN and the RCM will have little knowledge of the minority of registered nurses and midwives who belong to UNISON. Given RCN and RCM reluctance to recruit the non-registered nurses and midwives, they will find some difficulties in the constitution of FNC One.

As HCAs work through NVQ qualifications, tensions will arise between UNISON and the professional unions. UNISON may have a vested interest in flexibility at the expense of the professionals. This will tend to benefit unregistered staff, who will be seen by UNISON as their natural members.

Early compliance by the BMA with the JNC structure might give way to problems as they find themselves outvoted on issues.

They might use their strength to try to establish separate negotiating rights – in accordance with BMA national policy.

The professional unions tend to collect subscriptions through direct debit. Reference to deduction at source will be of little interest to them. Unions which support deduction at source will automatically supply membership information to management. Other unions may be reluctant to do this. There will also be differences of opinion in terms of negotiating tactics. Threats of industrial action will have meaning for some unions, but not for others. It is highly unlikely that trusts will accept the staff side 'no-industrial action' proposal – see below.

The staff side have proposed that it will elect a chairperson for each separate negotiation. Do they mean a chairperson of the staff side? A JNC does not usually have a chairperson. Do they mean a 'lead spokesperson' or equivalent? How will they identify, or define, a 'separate negotiation'?

Putting together procedural proposals is a relatively easy task. The unions will have had the experience of drafting and negotiating disciplinary, grievance, disputes and facilities agreements. In intra-organisational bargaining terms, these are relatively neutral, and rarely have discriminatory effects. The experience of working together in these areas no doubt created some joint problem-solving experience and abilities, which allowed them to formulate amicably the above draft. However it is unlikely that the unions are prepared for the divisiveness which will inevitably arise when they try jointly to agree on substantive issues. These, of course, will become more apparent as management respond both to their procedural proposals and, ultimately, their substantive proposals, and instinctively exploit these divisions.

### Inter-organisational Bargaining

This is concerned with the bargaining at JNC and FNC levels. The two drafts vary in terms of their proposals for the operation of the JNC. Assuming that the unions are united in their draft recognition procedure, what are the key issues which they will be faced with?

The disputes procedure has as its final stage a committee of the trust. In the unions' draft proposal there is a recommendation that disputes arising from the JNC and the FNCs may automatically go to conciliation/arbitration if not settled at trust level. This is a no-strike/industrial action clause. Will it be accepted?

There is a complete lack of clarity between the roles of the JNC and the FNCs. This problem of functional groups is obscured in the management draft by reference to 'particular groups'. Similarly management's exclusion of certain payments from trust-wide negotiations is wide open in terms of interpretation. This lack of clarity is a recipe for anomalies.

Do the staff side really want to be able to allow expert witnesses to appear at JNC level? Expert witnesses usually relate to consultation committees. Expertise should be drawn upon in adjournments. Management would probably resist the presence of experts, so if the unions are serious, they will need to muster some good arguments.

The above raises only a few of the issues. Students should be encouraged to identify others, track their possible future outcomes and try to predict what final bargaining arrangements are likely to look like. Role-playing the negotiating of the procedure will identify many of the problems. Students should be encouraged to reach agreement. What will certainly emerge is some understanding of the profound problems surrounding local negotiations in the context of the NHS.

**Case Study 2**

This case study relates to the negotiation of substantive issues linked to pay. The 1995 PRB award facilitating local bargaining led to immediate proposals from trusts. Whitley groups had already agreed an enabling clause for implementation in 1995–6. The following is a proposal put to the unions in March 1995.

Healthside NHS Hospital Trust

Offer to the unions (this does not apply to doctors, other than consultants, or to dentists).

1   The sum of any element of locally determined pay (the y factor) added to the nationally determined element of pay (the x factor) shall be the same for all groups of staff within an overall ceiling of 3 per cent.

2   For consultants the x factor will be 2.5 per cent. For all other groups it will be 1 per cent.

3   The y factor shall be linked to the performance of the Trust as whole and not to the performance of teams or individuals.

4   The x factor will be paid from 1 April 1995.

5   The y factor shall be paid as a lump sum in February 1996 subject to the achievement of performance targets specified in paragraph 6 below. These will be based on projections derived from performance during the months April 1995 to December 1995. The assessment of the achievement of the performance targets will be undertaken by the Chairman and Non-Executive Directors of the Trust Board.

6   The performance targets for 1995–6 shall be:

Achievement of a 6 per cent return on the net assets of the Trust as mandated by the Department of Health

Achievement of a 3 per cent efficiency target to include:

2.5 per cent increase in activity (1500 episodes) 0.5 per cent cash related cost improvement (£300 000)

Achievement of 95.8 per cent attendance target where 4.2 per cent represents sickness absence.

This second case could be used as a joint management/union negotiating exercise. Several points emerge. The unions will begin by seeking clarification of some of the points in the trust proposal. For example, will the lump sum, paid as the 'y' factor, be consolidated into salary? If not, why not? If so, when? All of the 3 per cent is being required as achievement from the workforce – has any inflation been allowed for in prices? Have the purchasers received any inflation funding from the government?

Will there be any independent auditing of the chairman and non-executive directors' decisions on performance? Given that the performance assessment is trust wide, what if some groups perform well and other groups do not? What incentive is there for doctors to perform if they are excluded? How important are the doctors? Performance could be affected by incompetent management. Revenue variations might be affected by factors unrelated to performance – prices might not meet contract requirements of purchasers, GP referral patterns might change.

How is activity measured? Are day cases, outpatient attendances, accident and emergency cases and in-patient cases reducible to single, weighted measures? Would a trust-wide scheme be better based on trust-wide financial indicators: for example, the ratio of labour costs to total income? What is the point of separating the 6 per cent return on capital assets? This could simply be treated as an overhead.

All of the above considerations should quickly lead to some understanding of the complexities of pay bargaining linked to performance indicators in the context of the NHS.

For the purpose of the exercise, an actual annual report of a hospital trust could be used and modified to match the £60 million budget implied above. It is possible to conduct an exercise very effectively without too much detail. However the following could be helpful, and treated as applicable to both exercises.

| Total Staff WTE 1965 | Trade union membership |
|---|---|
| Qualified nurses 572 | UNISON 38; RCN 423; none 192 |
| Midwives 122 | UNISON 8; RCN 14; RCM 103; none 11 |
| Unqualified nurses 228 | UNISON 151; none 123 |
| Admin & clerical 279 | UNISON 139; none 163 |
| Medical 183 | BMA 187 |
| Prof & tech 259 | UNISON 57; CSP 24; BDA 5; MSF 83; SoR 22; BOS 3; none 82 |
| Ancillary 279 | UNISON 193; GMB 16: none 94 |
| Estates 43 | UCATT 9; GMB 11; EETPU 7; UNISON 16 |

Note: union membership may exceed WTE (whole time equivalents) because of the number of part-time workers.

The budget for 1994–5 was distributed in the following way:

Non-pay: 32 per cent

Pay: 68 per cent:

> of which: Nurses and Midwives 29.9; Medical 14.2; Ancillary 6.4; Estates 3.4; A&C 6.5; P&T 5.3; Managers 2.2

The accounts only give sources of revenue in terms of the purchasers. For example, the Health Authority accounted for 73 per cent of the trust's income. Neighbouring authorities purchased another 2.5 per cent; GP fundholders purchased to the extent of 7.5 per cent; teaching and research contracts brought in 7.9 per cent, and other accounted for 9.9 per cent. This last item includes private patients, leasing of premises, car park charges and so on.

Those playing the management team might need to 'invent' consistent figures to 'fill out' some of the items. At the moment, published accounts are not incorporating revenues, or income, secured by specific specialisms, such as midwifery, for example.


### Conclusion

It is hoped that the material for the two case studies gives some life to the issues of local bargaining. Performance-related payments of the type incorporated in the second case study will open up a Pandora's Box of information demands from unions. Negotiators on both sides will find that this kind of bargaining will require considerable expertise, time and monitoring.

Tutors using these exercises should try to collect trust annual reports. These provide a wealth of information on revenues, expenditures, HRM policies, pay structures and clinical and medical activity.

# 11

# Pay and Flexibility in the NHS

This chapter is concerned with pay and flexibility in the NHS and some related issues not dealt with elsewhere in the text. As stated in Chapter 1, pay is estimated to account for approximately two-thirds of total NHS expenditure. Aspects of pay have already been dealt with in Chapters 3 and 4. The purpose of this chapter is to look at some of the issues associated with changes in the system of pay determination in the NHS.

OPCS (1995:70) states the following: 'The Government's objective throughout the service is progressively to introduce greater pay flexibility, to allow managers to relate pay rates to local markets and reward performance.' Local markets predominantly affect nursing, midwifery, ancillary, administrative and clerical, ambulance, and maintenance and works staff. The market for medical staff is very much a national and international market.

In an Executive Letter (EL(95)34), the NHSE Director of Human Resources and the Director of Finance and Corporate Information, wrote:

It is important to re-state the reasons for moving towards Local Pay. Local Pay:

gives employers greater control over 70% of their costs.

enables employers to design appropriate and flexible reward packages having undertaken a critical review of the work to be done and of roles and responsibilities.

is an essential part of developing NHS organisations as good employers recognising that high quality and cost effective services will only be achieved by a highly motivated staff.

The statements from both documents, if combined, produce a theory about the role of pay held by the government and the NHSE. That local pay bargaining gives employers greater control over their wage costs is an interesting proposition. If pay is to be related to the local labour market, then presumably the conditions of that market will dictate pay. Other things being equal, the assumption is that nationally determined rates produce higher average outcomes than local pay bargaining would, and that it is easier to exploit labour's weaknesses in a period of high unemployment through local pay determination. It follows from this, again other things being equal, that pay will tend to be lower for most NHS groups than it would have been under centralised bargaining.

In periods of high employment, centralised bargaining protects employers. It protects them from leapfrogging claims, and from competition between employers for scarce labour. In periods of low employment, centralised bargaining protects employees from having their pay forced down via the competition from unemployed labour. There is the possibility, clearly, that where labour shortages do arise, inflationary pressures might emerge. Although the general suggestion is that trusts are free to do their own deals, the NHSE still maintains a great degree of central control. NHSE control is reflected in its expression of views about what levels of overall increases in pay should be allowed. In 1995, it was stating that it did not expect average PRB pay rises to exceed 3 per cent in total, although individuals could be paid more. For consultants it set an average ceiling of 5 per cent. These objectives could be forced through by the NHSE/RO control of purchasers. Purchasers would challenge prices which incorporated higher than 'norm' wage increases. This exercise of control is best illustrated by a further extract from EL(95)34:

> The local pay increases for 1995–96 must be affordable. The context is that the Public Expenditure Settlement for HCHS revenue for 1995–96 gave a 1.3% real terms increase (4.5% cash). In addition, health services are expected to increase their efficiency by at least 3% (including savings from streamlining health authorities). HCHS prices inflation will be lower than the movement in general inflation because of savings to be delivered by the NHS Supplies Authority. This overall resourcing position allows scope both for increases in patient services of around 4% and for reasonable pay rises recommended by the DDRB and in the range expected by the NPRB.

There is thus scope for reasonable pay awards provided these are earned from the efficiency gains which all purchasers are required to secure.

Implicit in the above is a requirement that local bargaining will also be financed by productivity improvements. Probably the most important proposition in respect of devolvement is the proposal relating to 'a critical review of the work to be done and of roles and responsibilities'. Within a context of central funding control and central ordinances, along with centralised restructuring strategies, trusts are being asked, while taking advantage of local potential for lower pay, to 'secure wider changes in the design of jobs and in employee performance' (Brown and Walsh, 1994:p. 449). The chapter by Brown and Walsh from which this quotation is taken deals with pay generally in the UK. What this indicates is that the NHS is falling in line with other UK industries in its overall pay and jobs strategy. The implications at trust level would appear to be the following:

1. That pay scales reflect local market conditions for that part of the labour force which can be recruited locally.
2. That there be an element of pay which is based on performance.
3. That pay scales for various groups be linked to allow for flexible progression from one grade to another.
4. That the design of jobs be examined, using work study techniques and, if necessary, be restructured to meet service needs.
5. Implicit in the whole of the above is that there should be a search for greater workforce flexibility.

Much of this was summarised by the then NHSE Director of Human Resources, Ken Jarrold, in a *Guardian* interview (*Guardian*, 1995):

At one level, he says, it is illogical to continue paying a 'lead' of £425 a year to all psychiatric nurses and £165 to all geriatric nurses when there is no general problem recruiting them. There is no lead for theatre, casualty or renal dialysis nurses, where recruitment is difficult. More fundamentally, though, trusts are developing new types of job –

most commonly, health care assistants or support workers, but also nurse practitioners and paramedics – which do not fit into the Whitley structure.

## Local Markets

The same edition of the *Guardian* in its editorial suggests:

> a local element makes sense. It is absurd that the health authority in Blackburn, where rents are low, pays the same salaries as Bath, where rents are high. ...Even if there were no internal health market a national pay spine with flexibility to introduce local rates makes sense.

This misinterpretation by the *Guardian* allows for the clarification of some key issues. Rents in Blackburn could be low because people choose not to live there. This could mean that providers of essential services have difficulty recruiting certain types of labour. The concept of local labour markets being used to determine pay is not to compensate employees for variations in living costs, but to pay the lowest wage possible which is sufficient to recruit, retain and motivate staff. High rents or mortgages in certain markets may result in labour placing emphasis on job security as a factor rather than the pay level, particularly if there is no other job to go to.

Where types of labour are scarce employers may use a number of devices to try to solve the problem. One could be to offer higher pay than in other locations. Alternatives, which might avoid longer term-rigidity in terms of the pay structure, could be to offer pay supplements – London allowances have been a long-running example. These may be rationalised in terms of covering higher living costs in London, but this is not the explanation. There are many low-paid jobs in London without supplements. Paying attractive lump sums to join an organisation – 'golden handshakes' – is another method.

Jarrold's examples given above are related to national, rather than local, shortages or surpluses of labour. The logic of decentralised pay determination is that relatively immobile groups of workers, where there is relatively high unemployment, can be paid less than elsewhere. This, as suggested earlier, will affect such groups as nurses and midwives. Furthermore the objective is not to establish a national pay spine with local variations, as suggested by the *Guardian*, but to develop trust-based pay spines.

Some of the issues touched upon here were highlighted in a recent article in the *Health Service Journal* (1995). Trusts were allegedly concerned about the costs of local negotiations, and the possibilities of nearly 500 different sets of pay rates. It was felt that negotiations could possibly be tiered, with ancillary staff being dealt with at local level professional staff at regional level and expensive medical staff at national level. This latter point illustrates some of the concerns related to leapfrogging. Another problem with devolved bargaining is that wide variations across the country for professional groups, who see themselves as doing the same jobs, could lead to feelings of unfairness.

### 'To reward Performance'

It is not intended here to provide a detailed account of performance-related pay schemes and associated literature. For a succinct overview of these, see Kessler (1994). The purpose here is to discuss some current issues in respect of the NHS. Department of Health objectives, as indicated above, clearly include the extension of rewards related to performance. These can relate to individual, group or corporate (trust) levels of performance.

The issues are best illustrated through an example based on proposals from an actual trust. In this case the performance increments are linked to a combination of trust level and individual performance indicators. These have replaced automatic increments across most scales, although doctors and senior managers are excluded from this particular scheme. According to the scheme proposed by the trust, a percentage ranging from 0 per cent to 6 per cent of the minimum of each scale can be awarded depending upon the achievement of performance targets. Half of each annual award will be added to annual salary until the scale maximum is reached. The other half will be awarded as a lump sum and will be paid even beyond the scale maximum. For individuals who do not perform satisfactorily, the payments can be reduced by 50 per cent or be completely withheld.

Assessment of overall trust performance is made by the chairman and non-executive members of the trust board. The assessment is made against what are described as 'four key measurable performance criteria which the Trust needs to achieve to be successful in meeting the needs of patients'. These are described as:

1. Achievement of good quality standards such as those required by the Patient's Charter and purchaser requirements on maximum waiting times.
2. Achievement of the volume of patient episodes required by contracts with purchasers.
3. Achievement of the three financial requirements of the Trust ie balancing income and expenditure, achieving a 6% return on capital and meeting our external financing limit.
4. Achieving the developments of service set out in the Trust Business Plan.

Satisfactory performance of individuals is based on management assessment. The award of a half bonus would reflect performance which, if continued, would lead to a written warning. Examples of such performance are given as persistent short-term absence; persistent lateness or poor timekeeping; persistent errors, omissions or mistakes. The award of 'no bonus' would generally be expected to follow the award of a 'half bonus', where no significant improvement had followed. This would also be the case where performance had so deteriorated that a final written warning had been given.

There is a number of potential difficulties with the above system. The trust bonus depends upon factors which might vary as a consequence of forces well beyond the control of trust employees in particular NHSE and RO strategic objectives which have not been made public. This could lead to dissatisfaction. Furthermore assessment of performance against targets is in the control of the chairman and non-executive directors. Staff will feel that they have had no say in this assessment, and it could appear to be arbitrary. This in itself is divisive. It also produces the elements of divisiveness within the board, between executive and non-executive directors.

That 50 per cent of the bonus stops at the top of scales may create problems with staff in such positions. Given the criteria related to individual performance awards, all of which are linked to disciplinary issues, withholding of bonus introduces an element of 'double jeopardy'. Such cases will constitute a minority, and the system therefore creates little individual incentive. Kessler (1994) demonstrates the problems which arise from such schemes. Administration of the whole scheme appears to be immensely bureaucratic.

What is apparent from the above is that the system of rewarding performance is linked predominantly to pay increases with the major part of pay being dependent upon time at work and determined by the category of employment a member of staff is in. This is implicit in the notion of pay scales, which have a hierarchy. One way of rewarding performance is by granting movement up the hierarchy, by promotion. Movement up the hierarchy could be secured by accumulating additional skills and applying for jobs in the higher levels of the overall structure of pay scales.

Historically the NHS has had several hierarchies of pay scales, with separate ones for different types of workers. For example, there have been hierarchies for medical and dental staff, for nurses, midwives and health visitors, for professions allied to medicine, for ancillary staff and so on. All these scales overlap and provide a focus for internal comparisons. For example, in their evidence to the PRB for 1994, Nursing and Midwifery Staff Side (1993:36), it was stated: 'Comparisons betwen nursing sisters/charge nurses, midwives and junior doctors demonstrated that, despite overlapping roles, the pay of junior doctors was much higher.' This was seen to be 'unfair'. Perceptions of fairness are clearly important in the establishment of pay differentials. As suggested above, differentials based on performance will be perceived to be unfair if the methods of determining performance indicators and appraising performance are not seen to be appropriate. If managers are inconsistent in awarding bonuses, this will create discontent. Performance pay systems are extremely vulnerable to inconsistent application.

Professional groups in the NHS have been very critical of the use of performance indicators. They feel that health care is too complex to be reduced to quantitative measures of effectiveness and achievement. There is also the belief that they directly introduce financial incentives in a way which might jeopardise professional judgements. For example, a consultant who counsels a patient against minor surgery, and suggests a return visit to discuss a condition, might be tempted to save time and achieve a finished consultant episode (FCE) by undertaking the surgery against his or her judgement. FCEs are used as performance measures. (This is not a hypothetical case.)

Differentials are often based on notions of the skills, qualifications and difficulties involved in certain jobs. The PRB example shows discontent where two scales in the same industry are being compared. Discontent may also arise within a scale.

### 'Flexible Progression Between Grades'

Staff in the NHS, as elsewhere, wish to see a fair pay structure with opportunities to progress within it. According to Brown and Walsh (1994:445)

> The management of the fairness of pay is of great importance for the achievement of satisfactory labour productivity. ...The fact that individuals on their own may be ambivalent and inconsistent in the ways they form conceptions of fairness does not prevent their collectively being marshalled into an orderly consensus. This is the purpose of job evaluation.

Chapter 4 made some reference to job evaluation in the NHS: that it was widespread, that the clinical grading scheme for nurses, midwives and health visitors did not conform to equal value legislation, and that trusts were implementing local schemes. The NHS Training Division (1995) has offered guidance on local pay determination. It includes within it a section on job evaluation. The introduction of job evaluation at trust level is identified as a possibility, with a link to what it calls 're-engineering the organisation': 'There will be little point in evaluating current jobs and creating a salary structure that solidifies existing activities if you are looking to create greater flexibility in the longer term.'

What is being sought is an opportunity to redesign jobs, by enlarging and enriching them, and creating greater possibilities for flexibility and job rotation. Flexibility could require that all jobs are placed on one hierarchy of pay scales – a single pay spine. This would require all jobs to be evaluated according to a single system, rather than having separate systems for different types of employees. There would be an underlying notion that progress up the scale was available from bottom to top. This only becomes feasible with the removal of demarcation lines between jobs. In essence, this is not practical in the NHS, given entry qualification requirements for many medical and clinical posts. Nevertheless a combination of NVQs and modular inputs from universities and other institutions could weaken some of the more artificial and historically determined barriers. This is the reasoning.

Although the NHSTD guidance points to dangers, it is radical in its approach. Job evaluation is being recommended as a method to be used in conjunction with workforce restructuring.

### Job Evaluation

The literature on job evaluation is voluminous, and many guides to the various approaches are available. Here we will focus on the method generally being introduced in those trusts moving towards trust-based job evaluation schemes. Not all are attempting completely integrated schemes, and BMA policy, currently opposing job evaluation, makes this more difficult.

The main approach being used is that of 'points-rating'. In such a system, typical jobs, from related clusters of jobs, are chosen. These are described as 'benchmark' jobs. The idea is that each of these jobs is representative of a distinguishable category of employee: for example, midwife, nurse, auxiliary, porter, health visitor. Detailed job descriptions are secured, usually on the basis of a set of questions linked to predetermined factors. Factors identified are presumed to apply across the range of jobs, and represent essential elements or aspects of the job to be performed. For example, some jobs need qualifications and experience to be brought by a job holder, and the amount of either or both can vary. Some jobs carry more responsibility, require physical effort, or are carried out in difficult working conditions. The idea is that jobs can be ranked according to the 'quantity' of these factors required in order for the job to be performed adequately.

One scheme developed in the NHS in anticipation of the proliferation of trust-level job evaluation is known as Medequate –

developed by KPMG Management Consulting and Central Manchester Healthcare Trust. The factors on which this scheme is based are shown in Table 11.1.

TABLE 11.1   *Medequate*

| Factor | No. of levels | Score multiplier | Maximum Factor score | Weights (%) |
|---|---|---|---|---|
| 1 Qualifications/formal training, skills and experience | 8 | 10 | 80 | 8.7 |
| 2 Experience in post | 4 | 5 | 20 | 2.2 |
| 3 Communication | 6 | 15 | 90 | 9.8 |
| 4 Extent of advisory role | 8 | 15 | 120 | 13.0 |
| 5 Sensitivity | 5 | 15 | 75 | 8.2 |
| 6 Patient/client care | 3 | 5 | 15 | 1.6 |
| 7 Human resources management | 11 | 10 | 110 | 12.0 |
| 8 Financial resources management | 13 | 10 | 130 | 14.1 |
| 9 Asset management | 7 | 5 | 35 | 3.8 |
| 10 Judgemental skills | 7 | 15 | 105 | 11.4 |
| 11 Freedom of action | 6 | 10 | 60 | 6.5 |
| 12 Innovation and developmental skills | 5 | 5 | 25 | 2.7 |
| 13 Workplace | 4 | 5 | 20 | 2.2 |
| 14 Physical effort | 3 | 5 | 15 | 1.6 |
| 15 Pressure and unpredictability | 4 | 5 | 20 | 2.2 |

The list of factors is elaborated upon within the scheme. For example, each level of each factor has a definition. Level 8 qualifications will include the highest level of academic achievement. 'Financial resources' has levels based on the value of financial resources the job requires responsibility over. Each factor has a weighting related to what is considered to be its relative importance – these are listed in column three. The fourth column gives the total number of points achievable under each factor – column two times column three. Column five shows the optimum percentage of possible total points that could be scored attributable to each factor. This gives a measure of their relative importance as seen within the scheme. Column four gives the actual weights allocated to each factor.

The list of factors produced by this scheme is little different from the list of factors one would find in points-rating job evaluation schemes used in other parts of industry. There is a reference to patient/client care – the use of the word 'client' indicating something of the tenor of NHS changes – but this secures minimal weighting in the scoring system used above. The scheme does allow trusts to vary the weightings. Manipulating the weightings will allow trusts to secure the job hierarchy they think is appropriate if they decide to use the scheme. In other words the hierarchy of jobs is not determined by the scheme. The trust decides on the hierarchy it would like and then ensures that the factor weightings it chooses produces this.

Obviously the hierarchy of jobs will be based on the points allocated to each job in accordance with the scores they receive on each of the factors. If we were to assume a pay spine ranging from one to 90 points, it would be possible to imagine this as being divided up into 15 parts, each with six points. Each of these 15 parts could be called a grade, and jobs allocated to each of these grades. There would be scope for some choice of positioning within each grade, given the range of six points. Each grade would have a minimum and a maximum point. Pay levels could be allocated accordingly, with a minimum and maximum rate for each grade, and therefore for each job within each grade. Progression within the grade could then be allowed – perhaps on the basis of the case referred to above.

Whether this job and pay hierarchy will be perceived as fair by those affected is a separate question. No doubt trusts will try to use it to secure some of the flexibilities in the pay spine referred to above. Time will put pressures on the system, depending upon the extent to which staff use their different sources of power to achieve their separate objectives as jobs change in content. This latter point can be related to the notion that, as jobs change, or are 'redesigned', they may need to be re-evaluated. Usually some kind of appeals procedure is established. Given that evaluation is based on detailed job descriptions, changes in such can lead to appeals. This could create a situation where staff become less flexible, and management are reluctant to change job content, because of the impact of re-evaluations. A growing recognition by NHS managers that job evaluation can create inflexibilities is an important consideration and no doubt partly explains the slow take-up of schemes.

## 'Re-designing jobs'

Trust structures will continue to be affected by changes in levels and types of activities. These may reflect changes in demand, new technology and merger activities. Merger activities may lead to job losses, they may also lead to job reorganisation. Many trusts have contracted out services. This is reflected in a drop of over 50 per cent in the numbers of ancillary staff employed in the NHS during the last ten years. Restructuring of this type has repercussions in terms of types of jobs.

The 'Calman Report' (1993), which included consideration of junior doctors' hours and contained a recommendation to reduce them, has had an impact on the number of medical posts and created needs to offset the reduction in hours following this. 'Changing childbirth' requires an examination of the use of midwifery staff, implying greater flexibility in their use and an increased emphasis on community midwifery. This affects the use of GPs and obstetricians.

Skill mix analysis and work profiling have already been referred to in earlier chapters. Many trusts have been using basic work study techniques to redesign jobs and to alter the mixes of skills in departments or on wards. This process is best seen in terms of control and cost cutting rather than in terms of job enrichment and associated rhetoric.

## 'Greater Workforce Flexibility'

Securing a flexible use of the workforce has always been a management concern. Presumably it would be helpful to them if they could hire exactly the right numbers and quality of labour exactly when they wanted them. Just-in-time production has already been referred to. It was suggested then that it was more appropriate to think in terms of optimum utilisation of resources. There is an optimum use of labour, although in any particular situation it will be hard to identify what precisely this is. (Skill mix and job design are clearly linked to this.)

Harper (1993) describes one of the main purposes of her publication as being: 'To help local management (in NHS provider units) to improve its efficiency by providing a measure of labour performance.' This introduces another concept: *efficiency*. There is generally a presumption that everybody knows what this means. According to Harper, her measure of labour efficiency is *staff costs per unit of output*, unit labour costs (ULCs). On occasions ULCs are used in the same text to describe labour *effectiveness* and labour *performance*. These are quite different concepts. Costs per unit of output require a standardised measure of output if these are to be comparable over time or between trusts.

A difficulty in the NHS is that measuring the quality of any so-called 'unit of output' is extremely problematic. Because of this, comparisons of ULCs across units or over time or between units will always be contentious. Nevertheless, regardless of the issues relating to what exactly is being measured, it is obvious that labour might be used in such a way that, other things being equal, an alternative use might produce the same output at lower cost. ULCs could be improved (in Harper's terms) simply by forcing down labour costs by taking advantage of local labour markets. There is a whole range of ways of reducing ULCs, as has already been indicated.

The growing emphasis on flexibility in the use of the labour force in the NHS is linked to the desire to reduce labour costs. This emphasis also reflects what is happening in the wider economy. What follows is an attempt to identify aspects of labour flexibility which in recent years have been given some emphasis.

*Numerical Flexibility*

This is concerned with being able to vary the actual size of the labour force employed to deal with fluctuations in supply and demand. It could involve the use of part-time and temporary labour, short-term contracts and even subcontracting. The decline in ancillary staff employed in the NHS has already been referred to. For nursing and midwifery, in particular, bank staff or agency staff might be used on an 'on-call' basis.

To some extent, this trend, based almost solely on cost savings, conflicts with mission statements about loyalty, employees being valued assets, concepts of employee development and teamworking. This kind of flexibility can result in insecurity and loss of entitlements, such as those associated with pensions, holidays and other benefits, for staff subjected to it. Presumably the whole of a unit could be put out to tender and subjected to management contracts.

### Functional Flexibility

This form of flexibility involves staff performing a wider range of tasks, rather than being specialised. Chapter 3 referred to notions of demarcation lines, and restrictive practices amongst professionals. The use of NVQs and HCAs is linked to functional flexibility. Making nursing and midwifery staff flexible as between community and hospital is an example of functional flexibility. Obviously an objective is to ensure that labour is never idle, and thus be able to operate with lower staffing levels.

### Reward Flexibility

This relates to introducing more flexible systems of reward. Performance related pay has already been mentioned. Time off, privileged access to health care – almost anything could be considered. Items such as cars, holidays, free meals or creches could all be costed and employees then be allowed to choose up to the value of their salary.

Absenteeism is seen to be a large problem in the NHS. Rewards for attendance have been introduced by some trusts as a way of overcoming this. Other trusts have linked performance-related pay to reducing absenteeism levels. The problem with the latter is that one person's absence can affect another person's pay. NHSE (1995) gives several examples of rewards linked to attendance. One trust entered staff with 100 per cent attendance records into a draw for air miles. It has already been suggested that one problem with a wide range of rewards is that of administration of the pay system.

### Temporal Flexibility

This is concerned with the hours spent at work. A major objective of the employer is to have staff available when required. Temporal flexibility differs from numerical flexibility to the extent that it is concerned with short term variations in demand for the organisation's product or service. Overtime could deal with some upward variations, but this can be costly. It may not be able to deal with downward variations.

Fluctuations might be seasonal: it could be possible to close some hospitals, or parts of them, in summer. Other than fixing holiday periods, which might be insufficient to the purpose, annual hours contracts might be used. Employees may be required to complete a number of hours during a year, with perhaps ten-hour days in some parts of the year, and extended periods of absence in other parts. Variations in work pressure during each day could be dealt with by using compressed working weeks – three 12-hour days for some staff. For example, if a peak period is 10.00 hours to 22.00 hours, two staff might work that shift, with one staff working 01.00 hours to 13.00 hours and another 13.00 hours to 01.00 hours.

On-call payments in the NHS have always existed as one form of flexibility in terms of hours. Whether or not these should be incorporated into salary is a matter of judgement. Different pay rates for different shifts – payments for unsocial hours – can inhibit staff flexibility. Shift rotation is a way of standardising payments for hours worked, regardless of when they are worked.

### Conclusion

This chapter has overlapped many of the other chapters in this book. There is a considerable amount of material now emanating from the NHSE and trusts which indicates an interest in all the issues referred to. Whitley and the PRB system have essentially been disposed of by being rendered virtually meaningless. Local bargaining is producing a variety of initiatives in all the areas referred to. So far, there is insufficient research available to quantify for the NHS the extent of the growth of various forms of flexibility. What can be said with some certainty is that the traditional systems of pay and employment in the NHS are now in a process of radical change. Flexible pay, based on local conditions, will have effects on quality and training, especially amongst professional groups which have traditionally emphasised national standards and norms. The drive towards local bargaining must be seen to be associated with all the factors referred to in this chapter. Pay is only one element in such bargaining.

# Appendix: The National Health Service

The purpose of this appendix is to provide the general reader with some background to the history and structure of the NHS which might help to clarify some of the issues in the main body of the text.

## History

The NHS came into being on 5 July 1948, two years after the National Health Service Act had been passed. It marked the culmination of a process of developments in public health policy, ultimately brought to a head by the Second World War, and crystallised in the Beveridge Report (1944). According to Pimlott (1992:75), 'The Beveridge Report became the main pillar of the post-war Welfare State.' The White Paper, *A National Health Service*, (HMSO, 1944:47), stated the objectives of the NHS. These included universal access to the best medical and allied services available, and the provision of these through a comprehensive service and free of charge. It also stated that the promotion of good health, as well as the treatment of bad, was an objective. The service was to be financed through taxation.

There was opposition to the proposals, both to the principles involved and to the administrative structure proposed. This need not detain us. The key point was that the NHS on its inception contained these principles. Health is, of course, a highly sensitive area and the NHS can be conceived of as a socialist-style enterprise undermining individual responsibility or as a natural and ethical way of providing a commodity which is of central importance to people's lives. As such, it constitutes a major arena for the clash of political ideologies. The nature of health care also attracts into its employment people with a sense of dedication and commitment.

According to Lawson (1992:613) 'The National Health Service is the closest thing the English have to a religion, with those who practise in it regarding themselves as a priesthood.' This strength of feeling, which can probably be extended to the UK in general, has to be taken into account in analysing reactions to reform. Linked to this is the scale and cost of the NHS (see Table A.1) A part of the early history of the NHS

TABLE A.1   *Revenue allocations to regional health authorities* (in £ million)

| Region | 1994–5 Adjusted baseline for 1995–6 allocations[1] | 1995–6 Allocations if based fully on weighted capitation[2] | 1995–6 Actual allocation for spend on resident population[3] | 1995–6 Initial cash limits[4] |
|---|---|---|---|---|
| Northern & Yorkshire | 3 050.4 | 3 150.2 | 3 184.6 | 3 186.4 |
| Trent | 2 089.6 | 2 191.4 | 2 181.5 | 2 221.1 |
| Anglia & Oxford | 2 091.5 | 2 236.5 | 2 183.5 | 2 213.2 |
| North Thames | 3 402.1 | 3 499.1 | 3 551.8 | 3 784.1 |
| South Thames | 3 190.4 | 3 383.9 | 3 330.8 | 3 433.5 |
| South & West | 2 829.1 | 2 946.1 | 2 953.5 | 2 980.2 |
| West Midlands | 2 335.8 | 2 399.6 | 2 438.5 | 2 417.8 |
| North West | 3 064.7 | 2 217.1 | 3 199.6 | 3 255.2 |
| *England* | *22 053.6* | *23 023.9* | *23 023.9* | *23 491.8* |
| Sums not yet allocated, including central budgets | | | | 1 046.4 |
| Total net current cash limits | | | | 24 538.2 |
| Current spending to be financed by receipts (subhead AZ(1),(3) (part) and (4)) | | | | 35.4 |
| Total gross current provision (subhead A1) | | | | 24 573.6 |

*Notes:*
1. 1994/5 allocation for resident population including in-year adjustments and transfers.
2. The weighted capitation formula has been modified in the light of a review of weighted capitation.
3. 1995/6 basic allocation for resident population.
4. 1995/6 basic allocation plus general medical services cash limited expenditure and other adjustments.
*Source:*   OPCS (1995).

was the view that its impact on health would be such that improvements would ultimately reduce the cost of health care provision as the population was made healthier. This has been contradicted by the unlimited notion of what constitutes health, and what appears to be an unlimited demand for its provision. It is possible that part of its success has been that people live longer, but an older population generates additional demands.

What follows from the above is that reforms emanating from different governments will create strong reactions. For the Conservative government, the 'priesthood' consists predominantly of the professionals, who will obstruct changes designed to improve efficiency, and who will rationalise their vested interests in ethical and moral terms (see Chapter 4). Conservative reforms will be interpreted as attempts to undermine welfare and socialist based provision by privatisation. Because the costs are high, governments will be looking for reforms which reduce these.

A standard position taken by commentators is encapsulated by Lawson (1992:614). 'The National Health Service, although remarkably success-

FIGURE A.1 *NHS (UK) spending as % of GDP*

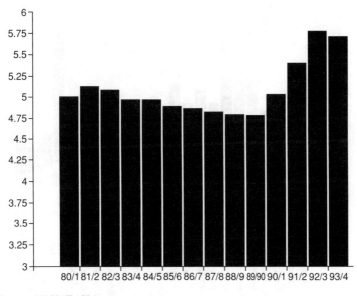

*Source:* NAHAT 1994.

ful by international standards in terms of straightforward cost control, was in many respects highly inefficient and fundamentally flawed.' Later (p. 616) he tells us that comparatively, in terms of health outcomes, 'the Health Service was in fact serving us pretty well'. He reaffirms the often stated position of his party, that it has no intention to privatise the NHS. However they do believe that people should have free access to private practice. The question at issue here is whether or not private practice can exist without crowding out a free service. Lawson's position seems to be that the NHS is inefficient but more efficient than alternatives abroad. The debate is replete with such contradictions.

What can be said is that the current reforms are a mixture of cost control, generating more effective outcomes, reducing the burden of taxation and passing the costs as far as possible to individuals as consumers, all underpinned by a faith in market mechanisms, which, it is believed, can be simulated in those areas funded by government. Not surprisingly, there has been a history of attempted reforms, all with a high profile, and impinging on HRM issues. Resistance to reform is inevitably expressed in terms of strong political and moral principles.

FIGURE A.2   *Percentage of GDP spent on public and private health care, 1989*

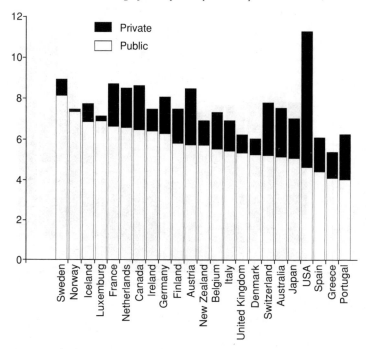

*Source:*   NAHAT 1994.

Here we are concerned with the most recent reforms which have generated the present structure of the NHS.

## The 'Griffiths' Reforms

The Griffiths Report (Griffiths, 1983) was not implemented in full. However it did result in important changes in the management structure. A central proposal was that there should be a clear management structure with accountability. This reflected the view that in the NHS 'there has been an absence of active, integrated management. The notion of a chief executive officer is central to the management of any giant corporate structure' (Strong and Robinson, 1988:4). At the time, the management of the district was in the hands of a team consisting of a medical officer, a consultant, a chief nurse, a representative of consultants, a general practitioner and a treasurer and an administrator. Decisions were reached by consensus, with no individual taking overall responsibility. In all of this the medical profession remained the strongest force and dominated any 'consensus'.

Following the Report, Health Circular (84) (DHSS:1984) was issued, instructing health authorities to appoint general managers at every level of the NHS by the end of 1985. This required the appointment of regional, district and unit general managers. Although appointments from outside the NHS were encouraged, these turned out to be the minority: most appointments were from administration within the NHS. In the process all of the general managers were removed from coverage by Whitley terms and conditions. An element of performance-related pay was introduced, along with 'short-term' contracts. In many cases these contracts became three-year rolling contracts, which meant that at any particular point two years' notice of dismissal became the effective outcome – hence some of the large 'pay-offs' for incompetent managers.

Another element of Griffiths was also pursued. This was the attempt to persuade doctors to accept greater managerial responsibility. What became known as the 'resource management initiative' was introduced, with experiments in allocating budgets and management positions to medical and clinical staff. Implicit in the Griffiths Report was the notion that politics and management could be separated. At national level a supervisory board would transmit policy to a management board, responsible for the day-to-day running of the NHS. This partially mimicked the structure of a nationalised industry. While central funding continues, it will remain impossible to divorce management decisions from political implications. Closing a hospital on the grounds of inefficiency, and attempting to hold general managers as responsible, will always have limited credibility. At the time of writing, senior Conservative politicians are threatening revolt against hospital closures, holding the Cabinet and the Secretary of State for Health as responsible.

In 1988, a change at the centre took place, with the decision to establish the Department of Health, which was split off from the Department of Health and Social Security. Figure A.3 indicates the structure of the Department of Health.

The above is not a complete account of changes in the NHS to date. It has focused on explaining the introduction of general management as an important adjunct to understanding the structure as it is at the time of writing. This is reflected in Figure A.4, which indicates changes in the supervisory board structure. In terms of political and central control, only cosmetic changes have taken place. The real changes have been in policy, as suggested above in the introductory section.

FIGURE A.3  *Structure of the Department of Health*

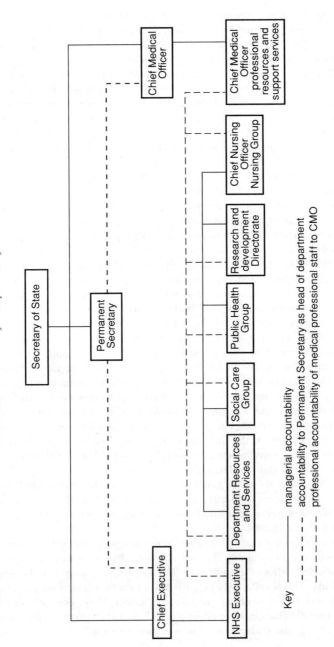

Key    ———— managerial accountability

– – – – accountability to Permanent Secretary as head of department

– – – – professional accountability of medical professional staff to CMO

*Source:*  OPCS (1995).

FIGURE A.4  *NHS structure*

**Structure of the NHS, 1995**

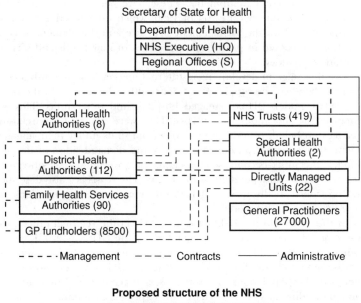

**Proposed structure of the NHS**

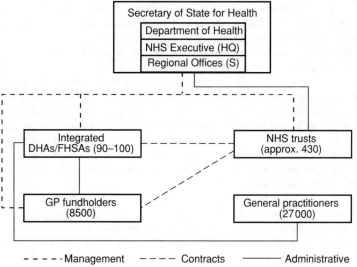

*Source:*  OPCS (1995).

## The Internal Market

It was indicated above that the general management structural changes represented major developments. These have been built upon by the NHS and Community Care Act of 1990, which introduced a notion of competition. Both the management structure and the element of competition are rooted in private sector notions of how goods and services should be provided.

The first stage in developing an internal market is to establish a clear division between the supply of and demand for the service. In the previous NHS model, DHAs managed hospitals and other units. This was financed by allocations from RHAs. They were, therefore, purchasing services on behalf of local populations from units under their management: they operated on both the supply and demand sides. In the new model, the units become self-managing or governing – self-governing trusts (SGTs) – independent of the DHAs. The trusts are also described as 'providers' in the new model. Private health care organisations are also providers in this model.

In the new NHS the DHAs are financed via the regional offices, the directors of these offices being members of the NHSE board. Regional offices are responsible for managing the performance of purchasers and trusts. Notionally funding is allocated to the DHAs on the basis of the needs of the populations they serve assessed according to demographic and morbidity factors. The DHAs are expected to identify the health care needs of their resident populations, and to satisfy these by negotiating suitable contracts with the providers. Regional offices are based on the areas indicated in Figure A.5.

Separating supply from demand has been reinforced by the establishment of GP fundholders (GPFs). GPFs agree to accept and manage a budget to cover their practice activity. They take responsibility for spending the budget on securing services for their patients directly from the providers. Becoming a GPF is voluntary. Part of the rationalisation behind this is that GPs are closer to understanding patient needs, and are likely to be effective purchasers. At the time of writing, GPFs account for less than 3 per cent of the value of purchases, although this varies between districts and from trust to trust. There are plans to greatly expand GP fundholding.

Following the above we have three groups of purchasers on the demand side: the DHAs, GPFs and private purchasers, whether corporate or individual. Most purchasing will come from within the district, although some will come from outside. This may involve patients travelling considerable distances to secure treatment. There are plans to encourage consortia of purchasers. On the supply side we have trusts and private hospitals and practitioners.

FIGURE A.5    *Boundaries for new RHAs and regional offices*

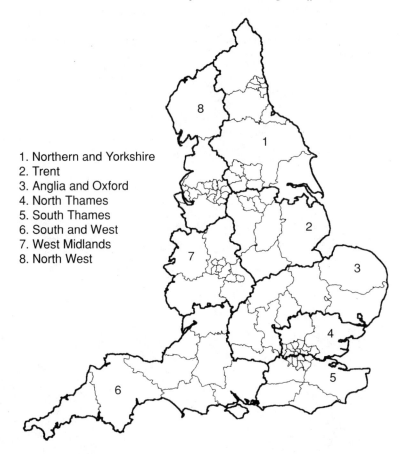

1. Northern and Yorkshire
2. Trent
3. Anglia and Oxford
4. North Thames
5. South Thames
6. South and West
7. West Midlands
8. North West

Based on FHSA boundaries.
Note: Since the map was drawn up the Health Secretary has agreed that East and West Cumbria should be part of a new Northern and Yorkshire Region, not the North West as originally proposed.
*Source:*    NAHT (1994).

It is not the purpose of this appendix to discuss the pure economics of the internal market. Our main concern is with HRM in the NHS. Obviously the drive to local pay determination is linked to competition. So also are subcontracting and compulsory competitive tendering. Trusts are not only self-governing, but free to opt out of national agreements linked to collective bargaining. The internal market fosters local pay arrangements. More importantly, it creates a new pressure on management to conform to centrally determined HR agenda via the leverage the NHSE has over the purchasers. These issues have been discussed in the main text.

# References

ACAS (1994) *Annual Report 1993*.

Armstrong, M. (1990) *A Handbook of Human Resource Management* (London: Kogan Page).

Bayer, R. (1988) *The Health and Safety of Workers; Case Studies in the Politics of Professional Responsibility*. (Oxford: OUP).

Beveridge, W. (1944) *Full Employment in a Free Society: A Report* (London: Allen and Unwin).

Blyton, P. and Turnbull, P. (eds) (1992) *Reassessing Human Resource Management* (London: Sage).

Bowen, David E. and Lawler, Edward E. (1992) 'Total Quality Orientated Human Resources Management', *Organisational Dynamics*, Spring.

Braverman, H. (1974) *Labor and Monopoly Capital* (New York: Monthly Review Press).

British Standards Institution (1969) *Glossary of terms used in work study* (London: BSI).

Brown, W. and Walsh, J. (1994) *Managing Pay in Britain* in Sisson (ed.).

Burchill, F. (1992) *Labour Relations* (Basingstoke: Macmillan).

Burchill, F. (1995) 'Professional Unions in the National Health Service', *Review of Employment Topics*, vol. 3 no. 1. August.

Calman, K. (1993) *Report of the Working Group on Specialist Medical Training* (Department of Health).

Carr-Hill, R., Dixon, P., Gibbs, I., Griffiths, M., Higgins, M. and McLaughan, D. (1992) *Skill Mix and the Quality of Nursing Care* (York: York University, Centre for Health Economics).

Casey, A.T. (1993) 'The New Deal at Rover', unpublished MA thesis, Keele University.

Clegg, H.A. (1979) *The Changing System of Industrial Realtions in Great Britain* (Oxford: Blackwell).

*Commission* v. *UK* (1994) IRLR 392, 412 (ECJ).

Cook, M. (1988) *Personnel Selection and Productivity* (Chichester: John Wiley).

Dale, B. and Cooper, C. (1992) *Total Quality and Human Resources; An Executive Guide* (Oxford: Blackwell).

Davies, P. and Freedland, M. (1993) *Labour Legislation and Public Policy* (Oxford: OUP).

Department of Health (DOH) (1992a) *Women in the NHS* (Lava: HMSO).

Department of Health (DOH) (1992b) *The Health of the Nation* (London: HMSO).

Department of Health (DOH) 1993 *Changing Childbirth* (Lava: HMSO).

DHSS (1984) Health Circular (84) 13, *Implementation of the NHS Management Inquiry Report*.

Dickens, L. (1994) 'Wasted Resources? Equal Opportunities in Employment', in Sisson (ed.).

Dyson, R. and Spary, K. (1979) 'Professional Associations', in N. Bosanquet (ed.), *Industrial Relations in the NHS* (King Edward's Hospital Fund for London).

EOC (1991) *Equality Management: Women's Employment in the NHS* (Manchester).

Fox, A. (1966) 'Industrial Sociology and Industrial Relations', *Royal Commission Research Paper No. 3* (London: HMSO).

Glascott, F. (1994) *Approaches to Pay by NHS Trusts* (Birmingham: NAHAT).

GMB (1994) *Human Resource Management*, training pack.

Gold, M. (1993) 'Innovative Teamworking in Europe', *European Participation Monitor*, no. 5.

Griffiths, R. (1983) *NHS Management Inquiry* (London: DHSS).

*Guardian* (1995) 'Peace hopes hang in the balance', David Brindle editorial, 19 April.

Guest, D. (1989) 'Personnel and HRM – can you tell the difference?', *Personnel Management*, January.

Harper, J. (1993) *Unit Labour Costs; A Guide – Revised Edition*, NHSME Personnel Development Division.

*Health Service Journal* (1995) 'Trusts moot massive pay shake-up', 20 April.

HMSO (1944) *A National Health Service*, Cmnd 6502 (London).

Hyman, J. (1992) *Training at Work* (London: Routledge).

Institute of Manpower Studies (1993) *Mapping Team Midwifery*, Sussex University.

IRS (1995) 'Managing Redundancy', *IRS Employment Review*, no. 580, March.

Kessler, I. (1994) 'Performance Pay', in Sisson (ed.).

King Edward's Hospital Fund for London (King's Fund) (1991) *The Work of the Equal Opportunities Task Force 1986–1990: A Final Report.*

Lawson, N. (1992) *The View from No.11; Memoirs of a Tory Radical* (London: Bantam Press).

Legge, K. (1989), *Human Resource Management: a critical analysis*, in Storey (ed.).

Lucio, M.M. and Weston, S. (1992) 'Human Resource Management and Trade Union Responses: Bringing the Politics of the Workplace Back into the Debate', in Blyton and Turnbull (eds).

Lyddon, D. (1993) *Mass Production in the Car Industry: A Flawed Concept and an Alternative History*, paper to Labour Process Conference.

Marchington, M. (1992) *Managing the Team: A Guide to Successful Employee Involvement* (Oxford: Blackwell).

Marginson, P. and Sisson, K. (1990) 'Single Table Talk', *Personnel Management*, May, 46–9.

McCarthy, W. (1976) *Making Whitley Work: A Review of the NHS Whitley Council System* (London: HMSO).

National Health Service Executive (1995) *VFM Update*, no. 3, March.

National Health Service Management Executive (NHSME) (1991) *Equal Opportunities for Women in the NHS.*

National Health Service Management Executive (NHSME) (1992) *Women in the NHS.*

National Health Service Management Executive (NHSME) (1993a) *Human Resource Survey.*

National Health Service Management Executive (NHSME) (1993b) *Ethnic Minority Staff in the NHS: A Programme of Action.*

National Health Service Training Division (1995) *Local Determination of Pay: Open Learning Materials.*

Newchurch Health Briefing (1993) *Strategic Change in the NHS,* August (Newchurch & Company).

Nichol, D. (1994) *Working Well in the NHS Conference Report,* Keynote Speech (NHSME).

Nursing and Midwifery Staff Side (1993) *Evidence to Pay Review Body.*

Oliver, N. and Wilkinson, B. (1992) *The Japanisation of British Industry: New Developments in the 1990s* (Oxford: Blackwell).

OPCS (Department of Health and Office of Population Censuses and Surveys) (1995) *Departmental Report* (London: HMSO).

Pimlott, B. (1992) *Harold Wilson* (London: Harper Collins).

Phelps Brown, H. (1986) *The Origins of Trade Union Power* (Oxford University Press).

Rose, M. (1988) *Industrial Behaviour* (London: Penguin).

Seifert, R. (1992) *Industrial Relations in the NHS* (London: Chapman & Hall).

Sisson, K. (ed.) (1989a) *Personnel Management in Britain* (Oxford: Blackwell).

Sisson, K. (1989b) 'Personnel Management in Transition?', in Sisson (ed.).

Sisson, K. (ed.) (1994) *Personnel Management; A Comprehensive Guide to Theory and Practice in Great Britain* (Oxford: Blackwell).

Storey, J. (ed.) (1989) *New Perspectives on Human Resource Management.* (London: Routledge).

Storey, J. (1992) *Developments in the Management of Human Resources* (Oxford: Blackwell).

Storey, J. and Sisson, K. (1993) *Managing Human Resources and Industrial Relations* (Buckingham: Open University Press).

Strong, P. and Robinson, J. (1988) *New Model Management: Griffiths and the NHS* (University of Warwick).

Tombs, S. (1990) 'Industrial Injuries in British Manufacturing Industry', *The Sociological Review,* vol. 38, no. 2.

Torrington, D. and Hall, L (1991) *Personnel Management: A New Approach* (London: Prentice-Hall).

TUC (1994) *Better Safety Standards at Work* (London: TUC).

UKCC (1986) *Project 2000 – A New Preparation for Practice* (London: UKCC).

Waite, R.K., (1991) *Manpower Planning and Healthcare Labour Markets* (University of Sussex: Institute of Manpower Studies).

Walton, R. and McKersie, R. (1965) *A Behavioral Theory of Labor Negotiations* (New York: McGraw Hill).

Webb, B. and Webb, S. (1897) *Industrial Democracy,* 1920 edn (London: Longmans, Green and Co.).

Webb, B. and Webb, S. (1917) Special Supplement on Professional Associations (Part 11), *The New Statesman,* 28 April.

Whyte, William H. (1960) *The Organisation Man* (Harmondsworth: Penguin).

Wickens, Peter K. (1993) *Lean Production and Beyond: The System, Its Critics and The Future* (University of Sunderland: Inaugural Professorial Lecture).

Wickens Peter K. (1994) Public Lecture, Keele University.

Womack, J.P., Jones, D.T. and Roos, D. (1990) *The Machine that Changed the World: The Triumph of Lean Production* (New York: Rawson Macmillan).

Woollard, F. (1954) *Principles of Mass and Flow Production* (London: Iliffe).

# Index